Hors d'œuvres On The Porch

Chef Jim Voltz

Seventy-five hors d'œuvre recipes organized
into fifteen complete party menus for easy entertaining
on the cottage porch or anywhere you enjoy
getting together with family and friends.

Printed in the United States of America

ISBN 978-0-578-07352-1

Illustrated by Chris Patterson

Thanks

Once again, thanks to so many friends who have supported me in so many ways during the writing of all three of my books.

Marjorie Elliott, partner, business manager and most of all friend, for all her hard behind the scenes work and support.

Nancy Myers, the best friend a person could ask for, always being there quietly giving her support.

Tim and Jeri Richardson for food tips, wine and drink suggestions and a quiet place to work with three furry friends.

Chris Patterson and her husband John; Chris for her continuing great art work and John who printed hundreds of digital photos for Chris so she could draw her wonderful detailed illustrations even when the Michigan snows covered everything in a deep blanket of white.

Betsie Hosick and Bob Weber for being such great friends and so generously providing their kitchen for a second season of Dinner on the Porch Cooking Classes.

Kim Fairchild, for his five recipes, foodie advice and great friendship.

Beth Tabbert, for her five recipes and a smile that brings a thousand others.

Priscilla Rush, for meticulously proofreading the draft copies.

It's very hard to include all those who have helped and supported me during endless hours of writing and preparing for my cooking classes. I remember and thank you all in my heart.

Jim Voltz

Contents

Introduction

"Hors d'œuvres on the Porch" continues the celebration of the many parties given on the porch of Sunny Shores, the little cottage I share with my best friend Nancy Myers on Crystal Lake near Frankfort, Michigan.

Even though Sunny Shores is one of the smallest cottages on the lake, about 800 square feet, we continue to have some of the largest parties throughout the summer. And now, with our new addition, we can entertain even larger groups. Last summer we added a 24 by 20 foot deck in front of the porch, allowing us, weather permitting, to have dinner out under the stars with our guests enjoying the sounds of the lake and woods.

I use the grill more often now that it's conveniently located on the deck and I can be near my guests while I cook. But what I like best is that the new deck allows us to have very large cocktail parties with a great atmosphere. We had a party for 60 guests last summer for Nan's birthday. I set the bar up on the deck and served the hors d'œuvres on the screened-in porch which eliminated any problem with bugs and got people to move around and mingle during the party. It worked beautifully and gave me the idea for this cookbook's title, "Hors d'œuvres on the Porch."

Separating the drink area from the food area works well for just about any cocktail party. As I mentioned, it gets people moving around and makes for easier access to each area. For cocktail parties, especially those at or near the dinner hour, I typically serve at least five different hors d'œuvres allowing three of each per guest. This way guests can eat as much or as little as they want; giving them the option to go on to dinner afterwards or to make this their full meal.

I rarely serve dips at my parties because you always find dip and broken pieces of crackers on the floor after the party. And, to make it easier for the guests, I prefer that every hors d'œuvre is truly finger food; no forks, knifes, or spoons required.

When planning your party, remember presentation is a big part of anything you eat. It doesn't have to be elaborate, but a little color and texture can make the simplest thing you serve into something that no one will forget. Spend a little time decorating not only your hors d'œuvres (I've included several ideas for garnishes throughout the book) but the space where you will present them. Use anything you have around the house, such as flowers and herbs from your garden and a favorite object, like an old family vase or bowl, to add your personal touch to the event. A really simple but effective treatment for the hors d'œuvre table is to put a tablecloth on the table, place three or four sturdy boxes of different heights on top, then cover the boxes with different colored cloths. Place your various hors d'œuvres on the covered boxes and some directly on the table. This will give depth and dimension, and more interest, to the table.

After you've setup the hors d'œuvre table, don't forget the bar area. Put a small bouquet on the table and a bowl of nuts for the drinkers to munch while fixing a drink. (I don't recommend mixed nuts as it encourages people to pick through them and take only the ones they like.)

All of the above can be done hours, or even the day before your party. As I've emphasized in my other two cookbooks, doing as much as you can ahead of time is one of the keys to a successful party. Two other disciplines I've stressed in the past are "mise en place" and the practice of reading all the recipes in your menu at least twice several days before your party. "Mise en place" is literally translated as "put in place" and means simply organizing all required ingredients and utensils before you start cooking. It ensures that you won't waste time or become frustrated looking for something, or worse yet, discover you don't have a critical ingredient while in the middle of preparing a recipe. Incorporate these three simple disciplines into all your party preparations and I promise that you will find entertaining so much easier and less stressful.

This book is organized into fifteen chapters. Each chapter contains a complete cocktail party menu with recipes for five hors d'œuvres, a special cocktail drink, and wine suggestions that complement the menu. There is also a beautiful original drawing by Chris Patterson at the beginning of each chapter and a short story about some of the delightful people who have been guests on Sunny Shores' porch or part of my cooking classes.

You can use each chapter as a total cocktail party or mix and match items to your liking. If you study the menus closely, you will notice that many contain a mix of recipes that could be expanded into a complete dinner party with an appetizer, main course, and dessert. Most of the hors d'œuvres can be prepared in advance, again enabling you to take a break ahead of the party and allowing you to be part of the event. Enjoy.

Chef Jim

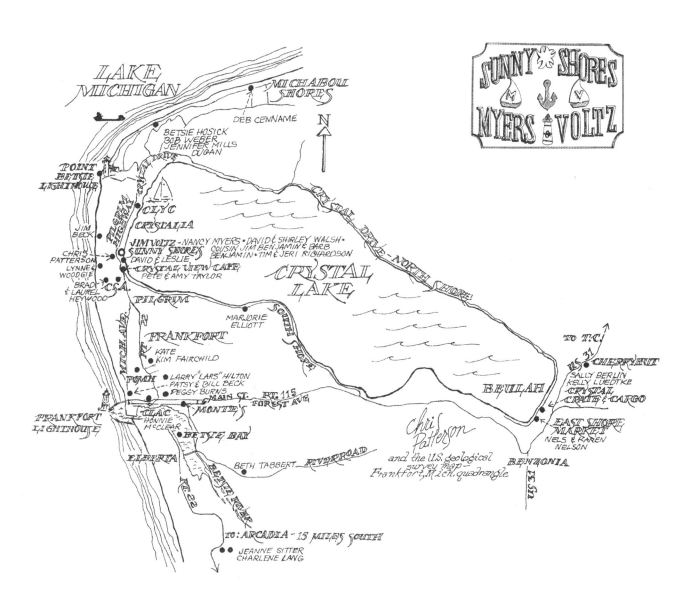

LAKE MICHIGAN

MICHABOU SHORES

DEB CENNAME

BETSIE HOSICK
BOB WEBER
JENNIFER MILLS
DUGAN

N

POINT BETSIE LIGHTHOUSE

CRYSTAL DRIVE

CRYSTAL DRIVE - NORTH SHORE

CLYC
CRYSTALIA

JIM BECK

PILGRIM HIGHWAY

JIM VOLTZ · NANCY MYERS · DAVID & SHIRLEY WALSH ·
CHRIS PATTERSON
LYNNE WOODGIE
SUNNY SHORES   COUSIN JIM BENJAMIN & BARB
DAVID & LESLIE   BENJAMIN · TIM & JERI RICHARDSON
CRYSTAL VIEW CAFE
PETE & AMY TAYLOR

CRYSTAL LAKE

BRAD & LAUREL HEYWOOD

CSA

PILGRIM

FT. 22

MARJORIE ELLIOTT

SOUTH SHORE

FRANKFORT

MICH AVE

KATE
KIM FAIRCHILD

TO T.C.

U.S. 31   CHERRYHUT

SALLY BERLIN
KELLY LUEDTKE

POMH   LARRY "LARS" HILTON
PATSY & BILL BECK
PEGGY BURNS   FT. 115

MAIN ST.   FOREST AVE.

BEULAH

CRYSTAL CRATE & CARGO

FRANKFORT LIGHTHOUSE

CLAC
HONNIE McCLEAR   MONTE'S

BETSIE BAY

EAST SHORE MARKET

NELS & KAREN NELSON

ELBERTA

BETSIE RIVER

FT. 22

BETH TABBERT   RIVER ROAD

Chris Patterson
and the U.S. geological
survey map -
Frankfort, Mich. quadrangle

BENZONIA

US 31

TO: ARCADIA - 15 MILES SOUTH

JEANNE SITTER
CHARLENE LANG

SUNNY SHORES
MYERS VOLTZ

9

Sunny Shores Gets a New Addition and Bob Gets Braised Lamb Shanks

We have an exciting new addition to Sunny Shores, a deck that more than doubles our space for entertaining; as long as the weather cooperates. Ted Liakopoulos, a local carpenter, was in charge of the project and designed the structure to hold crowds of people and save the lovely Cedar tree that now grows up through the middle. Several friends helped with construction, but it was Bob Weber who probably contributed the most. He was over nearly every morning at 8:00 and worked through the day. This made it impossible for anyone else who happened to be at the cottage not to pitch in as well. How could anyone sit around while Bob, our favorite octogenarian, slaved away on a hot summer day? Our deck became a neighborhood project. I made braised lamb shanks for Bob for dinner one night in appreciation. Bob says it's one of his favorite dishes and he never finds it on restaurant menus anymore.

The crab and shrimp puffs in this menu are one of the hors d'œuvres I served for Nan's birthday party which was our first party on the new deck. I'd never tell how old Nan is, let's just say I met Nan more than a few years ago in swimming class when I was five and she was four. We've been best friends ever since.

Menu I

Hors d'œuvres On Deck
(Serves 8)

Stilton Roll-Ups

Pineapple & Cheese Kabobs

Crab & Shrimp Puffs

Tomato Aspic in Cucumber Boats

Mini Onion Sandwiches

Scotch Bairn Cocktails

I love this grouping of hors d'œuvre recipes. It encompasses a wide variety of flavors and textures and makes a spectacular presentation on a buffet table. You don't need much decoration for the table as the food itself will create the atmosphere and whet the appetite of your guests.

Stilton Roll-ups

12 oz cream cheese

4 oz Stilton Bleu cheese

2 Tbls dry sherry

$\frac{1}{4}$ tsp curry powder

1 bunch chives

Pineapple & Cheese Kabobs

1 large ($14\frac{1}{2}$ oz) jar or can pineapple chunks packed in syrup or natural juice

1 16-oz block sharp Cheddar cheese

Decorative toothpicks

Crab & Shrimp Puffs

4 oz lump crab meat

4 oz cooked salad shrimp

$\frac{1}{2}$ cup grated sharp Cheddar cheese

3 green onions

1 tsp Worcestershire sauce

1 tsp dry mustard

4 large eggs

1 cup flour

1 stick unsalted butter

Salt

Tomato Aspic in Cucumber Boats

3 English cucumbers

2 cups V-8 Vegetable Juice

1 lemon

2 packages unflavored gelatin

1 bunch chives

Mini Onion Sandwiches

2 loaves thinly sliced cocktail rye bread (you need 48 slices)

3 small red onions

Mayonnaise (about 2 Tbls)

1 stick unsalted butter

1 bunch parsley

Scotch Bairn Cocktails

Good scotch, like Glenlivet

Cointreau

Orange bitters

Stilton Roll-Ups
(Makes 24 pieces)

1. Put 12 oz room temperature cream cheese in food processor

2. Crumble 4 oz room temperature Stilton Bleu cheese on top

3. Add 2 Tbls dry sherry and $\frac{1}{4}$ tsp curry powder

4. Pulse until smooth, put in bowl, cover and chill for several hours or overnight

5. Roll into small balls about 1 inch in diameter

6. Roll balls in finely chopped chives and chill

Bring to room temperature before serving.

Pineapple & Cheese Kabobs
(Makes 24 pieces)

1. Drain 1 large jar of pineapple chunks and save liquid

2. Cut 16-oz sharp Cheddar cheese into 1 inch cubes

3. Place pineapple piece on toothpick, then a piece of cheese followed by another pineapple chunk

4. Place on serving tray, sprinkle with reserved pineapple liquid

Cover and chill until serving.

NOTES

Crab & Shrimp Puffs

(Makes 36 pieces)

1. Preheat oven to 400 degrees Fahrenheit

2. Combine the following in a large bowl:

    a. 4 oz lump crab meat, chopped

    b. 4 oz cooked salad shrimp

    c. $\frac{1}{2}$ cup grated sharp Cheddar cheese

    d. 3 green onions finely chopped
       (chop both white and green parts)

    e. 1 tsp Worcestershire sauce

    f. 1 tsp dry mustard

3. In a medium sauce pan, combine the following and bring to a boil:

    a. 1 cup water

    b. 1 stick unsalted butter

    c. $\frac{1}{4}$ tsp salt

4. Remove from heat and using a hand mixer,
   add 1 cup flour and beat well

5. Add 4 large eggs, one egg at a time,
   beating thoroughly after each addition

6. Using a spoon, thoroughly fold in the crab mixture.

(You can complete to this point and chill until ready to bake)

7. Drop by teaspoonfuls onto a nonstick baking pan

8. Bake for 15 minutes, reduce oven temperature to 350
   and bake 10 more minutes until golden

Serve warm or at room temperature.

Tomato Aspic in Cucumber Boats
(Makes 24 pieces)

1. Prepare aspic by adding 2 packages of unflavored gelatin to $\frac{1}{2}$ cup hot water and stir until gelatin dissolves, set aside

2. Heat 2 cups of V-8 Vegetable Juice in a pan until very hot, but not boiling

3. Add the gelatin mixture and the juice of one lemon

4. Reduce heat and cook for 5 minutes until mixture starts to thicken

5. Pour into 8x8x2 inch pan, cover and chill for 3 to 4 hours until firm or overnight

6. Wash and cut ends off 3 English cucumbers (you do not need to peel English cucumbers)

7. Cut each cucumber into 8 pieces about $1\frac{1}{2}$ inches thick

8. Using a melon baller take a small amount of pulp from the center of each slice

9. Sprinkle pieces with salt and put into a colander to drain for 2 to 3 hours

10. Put on paper towels to dry, do not rinse

11. Place cucumbers on platter and using a melon baller, scoop the chilled tomato aspic from pan and put into cucumber cavity, sprinkle with finely chopped chives

Keep chilled until serving.

Mini Onion Sandwiches

(Makes 24 pieces)

If you want to be really fancy, trim the crusts from the bread.

1. Spread 24 slices of thinly sliced cocktail rye bread with a small amount of mayonnaise

2. Spread another 24 slices with a small amount of unsalted butter

3. Thinly slice 3 small red onions and put a thin slice on the 24 slices with mayonnaise

4. Sprinkle onions very lightly with salt

5. Sprinkle onions with finely chopped parsley

6. Top with the buttered slice of bread

If not serving immediately, refrigerate then bring to room temperature before serving.

Scotch Bairn

(Per drink)

2 oz good scotch, like Glenlivet
½ oz Cointreau
2 dashes orange bitters

1. Put all ingredients in cocktail shaker with ice
2. Shake well and strain into cocktail glass, with or without ice

Wine and/or Beer

For this menu Tim recommends a pinot blanc
or dry sherry such as Tio Pepe or La Ina.
A brown ale or bock beer would also
pair nicely with the flavors here.

Beth Makes a Splash

Larry "Lars" Hilton and Beth Tabbert dropped by Sunny Shores one day last spring, not unusual except that Beth was soaking wet. When I saw there were two kayaks on the beach, I understood. I gave Beth a towel, some dry clothes, and listened to two versions of the same story. It seems that Lars had wanted to go kayaking on this cool day in early May and talked Beth into going.   Here's where the stories diverge.

According to Lars, it was a calm morning with just a slight breeze. After he and Beth got a ways down the lake, Lars turned around and could only see the bottom of Beth's kayak floating on top of the water. "I then saw that she was out of the boat and safe. I told her to leave the boat and wade ashore while I recovered her kayak and followed her in. I don't think I laughed," asserted Lars. Beth says not so. According to Beth it was windy on the lake and she questioned the wisdom of going. "After I tipped over, Lars kept yelling at me to wade ashore. Well, that might have worked for Lars who's over six feet tall, but at 4'10" I couldn't touch bottom.   It was a real struggle to get ashore and all I could hear was his laughter," says Beth.

I don't know why these two don't get married.

The recipes in the next menu were all provided by Beth. When Beth and Lars aren't kayaking, they like to cook and are very good at it. I just wish Lars could get Beth's recipe for pie dough, it's the best I've ever had but she won't give up the old family recipe.

Menu II

Make a Splash
(Serves 10 to 12)

Chopped Liver

Crabmeat Mold

Pecan "DIP" Spread

Mini Pasties with Sweet Picante Sauce

Italian Sausage & Pepper Spread

Manhattans

Beth Tabbert provided all the recipes in this menu and although I typically never serve dips and spreads, that doesn't mean I don't like them. The ones included here are all great and not too messy for my tastes. Her chopped liver recipe is very close to a recipe I got from my friend Ron's aunt which he says is an old traditional Jewish chopped liver recipe. We can always count on Beth to prepare something great and help Lars create one of his terrific desserts.

Chopped Liver

1 pound chicken livers

2 medium yellow onions

½ cup unsalted butter (1 stick)

3 large eggs

1 large sweet potato

1 French baguette

Salt and pepper

Crabmeat Mold

2 8-oz packages cream cheese

8 oz real crabmeat

1 cup chili sauce

1 lemon

1 Tbls Worcestershire sauce

1 tsp prepared horseradish

1 Tbls grated yellow onion

1 French baguette

1 Tbls olive oil

Salt

Pecan "DIP" Spread

2 8-oz packages cream cheese

1 cup sour cream

5 oz dried beef

1 small green bell pepper

1 small yellow onion

2 cloves fresh garlic

¼ cup (½ stick) unsalted butter

1 cup chopped pecans

Plain bagel chips

Mini Pasties with Sweet Picante Sauce

1 10-oz can buttermilk biscuits

1 large egg

1 Tbls olive oil

5 oz ground beef or turkey

1 small red potato

1 small yellow onion

1 small rutabaga

2 garlic cloves

½ cup shredded Cheddar cheese

¼ cup prepared picante sauce

¼ cup ketchup

1 bunch fresh parsley

Salt and Pepper

Italian Sausage & Pepper Spread

1 pound sweet or mild Italian sausage (whole links, not bulk)

2 Tbls olive oil

1 medium green bell pepper

1 medium yellow bell pepper

1 medium red bell pepper

1 large yellow onion

1 large garlic clove

1 26-oz jar of prepared marinara sauce

1 cup dry white wine

2 French baguettes

Manhattan

Bourbon

Sweet Vermouth

Angostura bitters

Maraschino cherries

Chopped Liver
(Serves 10 to 12)

1. Hard boil 3 large eggs (see page 98 for hard boiling eggs), peel, cool, roughly chop and set aside
2. Boil one large sweet potato in salted water until soft, about 20 minutes, then cool, peel, roughly chop, and set aside
3. Roughly chop 2 medium yellow onions and set aside
4. Melt ½ cup (1 stick) unsalted butter in large skillet over medium high heat. Add onions and cook until soft, but not browned, about 5 minutes.
5. Rinse and drain 1 pound of chicken livers and then add to the onions and cook for about 10 minutes until no longer pink
6. Transfer liver and onion mixture to a food processor
7. Add the chopped eggs, sweet potato, 1 tsp salt and ½ tsp pepper and process until smooth

Cool and serve with baguette slices or toast points.

Crabmeat Mold
(Serves 10 to 12)

1. Combine 16 oz room temperature cream cheese with 8 oz of real crabmeat
2. Put mixture into a mold which has been lightly coated with olive oil and keep chilled until serving
3. Make the sauce by combining the following in a small bowl and keep chilled until serving:
    a. 1 cup of chili sauce
    b. 2 tsp freshly squeezed lemon juice
    c. 1 Tbls Worcestershire sauce
    d. 1 tsp prepared horseradish
    e. 1 Tbls grated yellow onion
    f. ½ tsp salt

To serve, unmold crab mixture onto a large platter, pour sauce over top and serve with baguette slices or toast points.

Pecan "DIP" Spread

(Serves 10 to 12)
(Remember I don't like DIPS, but this is not really messy)

1. Bring 16 oz of cream cheese to room temperature

2. Preheat oven to 350 degrees Fahrenheit

3. In a large bowl mix together:

    a. 16 oz room temperature cream cheese
    b. 1 cup sour cream
    c. 5 oz dried beef, diced
    d. ½ cup diced green bell pepper
    e. 1 small yellow onion, diced
    f. 2 cloves (approximately ½ tsp) of minced fresh garlic
    g. ½ tsp freshly ground black pepper

4. Spread mixture evenly into an 8x8 inch square, or 9 inch round, baking dish

5. Melt ¼ cup (½ stick) unsalted butter in a small pan

6. Take off the heat and add 1 cup chopped pecans and ¼ tsp salt and mix well

7. Spread the pecans evenly over the mixture in the baking dish

8. Bake for 20 to 25 minutes, until lightly browned

Serve warm or at room temperature with bagel chips and a knife to spread.

Mini Pasties with Sweet Picante Sauce
(Makes about 20 pieces)

1. Preheat oven to 400 degrees Fahrenheit

2. In a small bowl beat 1 large egg and 1 Tbls water together to create an egg wash and set aside

3. Heat 1 Tbls olive oil in a medium skillet over medium high heat, add 5 oz of ground beef (or ground turkey) and brown lightly

4. Add the following to the skillet:
    a. 1 small red potato, peeled (optional) and diced
    b. 1 small finely diced yellow onion
    c. 1 small rutabaga, peeled and diced
    d. 1 Tbls finely chopped fresh parsley
    e. $\frac{1}{2}$ tsp salt
    f. $\frac{1}{4}$ tsp freshly ground black pepper
    g. 2 cloves of garlic, minced

5. Reduce heat to low, cover and simmer until potato and rutabaga are fork tender

6. Take off heat and cool to room temperature

7. Separate the biscuits from 1 10-oz can of buttermilk biscuits, place on a lightly floured board, and cut in half

8. Roll each biscuit half into a 4 inch circle

9. Place equal amounts of the meat mixture over half of each biscuit circle

10. Sprinkle shredded Cheddar cheese over each biscuit circle

11. Fold over each biscuit to cover mixture, creating a semi-circle then crimp the edges together to seal and prick each pastie twice with a fork

12. Place pasties on a lightly greased cookie sheet. Brush the top of each pasty with the egg wash and bake for 8 to 10 minutes until golden

13. In a small bowl, mix $\frac{1}{4}$ cup prepared picante sauce and $\frac{1}{4}$ cup prepared ketchup

Put warm or room temperature pasties on serving platter garnished with parsley sprigs along with the picante sauce on the side.

NOTES

Italian Sausage & Pepper Spread
(Serves 12 Plus)

1. Preheat oven to 300 degrees Fahrenheit

2. Pierce the links of 1 pound of sweet or mild Italian sausage with a fork, place in a large pot and cover with water

3. Bring to a light boil over medium heat and cook for about 15 minutes until firm

4. Drain and cool

5. Cut the sausage into bite size pieces and remove skin by scoring each piece with a sharp knife

6. Place sausage pieces in a large baking dish

7. Heat 2 Tbls olive oil in a large skillet over medium high heat and sauté the following until tender, about 5 to 6 minutes, being careful not to overcook until mushy:

    a. 1 medium green bell pepper, cleaned and thinly sliced

    b. 1 medium yellow bell pepper, cleaned and thinly sliced

    c. 1 medium red bell pepper, cleaned and thinly sliced

    d. 1 large yellow onion, peeled and thinly sliced

    e. 1 large garlic clove, minced

8. In a large bowl, combine 1 26-oz jar of marinara sauce and 1 cup dry white wine and pour over sausage in baking dish

9. Top with the bell pepper/onion mixture, cover and bake for 1 hour

Serve warm or at room temperature with 2 thinly sliced baguettes (toasting baguettes is optional).

Manhattan
(Per drink)

2½ oz bourbon
¾ oz sweet vermouth
Dash of angostura bitters
1 maraschino cherry

1. Put bourbon, vermouth, bitters and ice in a shaker and stir gently (do NOT shake).

2. Strain into a chilled cocktail glass (ice optional)

3. Garnish with the maraschino cherry.

 # Wine

For the varied and rich flavors in this menu, Tim recommends an Italian Pinot Noir or a chilled Beaujolais which is slightly fruitier.

Jim and Monte Face Off Over Smoked Fish Pâté

Monte's Smoke House has been a Frankfort classic for years. My mother used to buy fresh fish and smoked chub there over thirty years ago, and now I shop there for both my dinner parties and my cooking classes. The owner, Monte Finkhouse, and I have become good friends as a result. Monte is often described as a bit of a character. His store hours can be somewhat "flexible," but don't try to call ahead, you won't find Monte's in the phonebook; he doesn't like phones and doesn't have one in his store.

A few years ago, Monte started carrying homemade smoked fish pâtés. They're quite good and very popular with his customers. As a little friendly "throw down challenge, " I took my smoked fish pâté in for Monte to try and we now have a running argument over whose is better. One thing Monte didn't appreciate was that when I demonstrated my pâté in a cooking class, I told my students to use just the tail section of the smoked fish; the tail section has very few pin bones to worry about. Now Monte says he can't sell the forward sections!

I've included my recipe for smoked fish pâté in the next menu. It's very easy; only two ingredients, but if that's even more than you want to do, I can recommend Monte's as a substitute.

Menu III

Throw Down
(Serves 8)

Betsie Bay Smoked Lake Trout Pâté

Sunny Shores Pigs in a Blanket

Puff Pastry Pizzas

Spicy Olives

Lychee & Pineapple Skewers

Gin Buck Cocktails

This menu has two items the kids will really like. The individual pizzas and the Lychee and pineapple skewers are perfect for them and the Sunny Shores pigs in a blanket will go fast if they like shrimp. The Betsie Bay smoked lake trout pâté and the spicy olives are meant for a more mature palate along with the Gin Buck Cocktail. I love gin but it does not like me, so one only please.

Shopping List

Betsie Bay Smoked Lake Trout Pâté

1 pound smoked lake trout

3 Tbls mayonnaise

1 jar bread and butter pickles

1 package wheat crackers

Sunny Shores Pigs in a Blanket

3 cans refrigerated crescent rolls

24 large cooked shrimp

1 small jar mango chutney

1 large egg

Puff Pastry Pizzas

2 sheets frozen (or refrigerated) puff pastry dough

12 cherry tomatoes

12 oz crumbled feta cheese

1 bunch fresh basil leaves

Spicy Olives

1 pound deli Spanish olives, pitted if possible (if you can't find deli olives, canned is ok)

½ cup white wine vinegar

½ cup extra virgin olive oil

1 bunch fresh chives

2 garlic cloves

2 tsp paprika

1 tsp black peppercorns

Decorative toothpicks

Lychee & Pineapple Skewers

3 14½-oz cans lychee nuts

1 large jar or can pineapple chunks in syrup or natural juice

1 bunch fresh mint

Long decorative toothpicks

Gin Buck

Gin

Fresh lemons (½ lemon per drink)

Ginger Ale

Straws

Betsie Bay Smoked Lake Trout Pâté
(Serves 6 to 8)

1. Filet one pound of smoked lake trout by removing the skin, bones and excess fat. Check carefully for any pin bones and remove any dark colored meat, use only the white meat.

2. Using your clean hands, or with latex gloves, flake the meat into a food processor, again checking for any pin bones.

3. Pulse the fish meat 4 or 5 times to create a coarse mixture.

4. Add 3 Tbls mayonnaise and pulse 4 or 5 more times until smooth.

5. Transfer to a serving dish, you can mold this mixture if desired.

Serve the pâté with crackers and a dish of bread and butter pickles. Or, to make it easier on your guests, put some pâté on each cracker and top with a small piece of a bread and butter pickle. This will also greatly cut down on the mess after the party – fewer broken crackers and globs of pâté on the floor.

This can be prepared one or two days in advance and kept cold. You can substitute any smoked fish for this recipe.

NOTES

Sunny Shores Pigs in a Blanket
(Makes 24 pieces)

1. Preheat oven to 375 degrees Fahrenheit

2. Unroll and separate the rolls from 3 cans of refrigerated crescent rolls onto a flat, lightly floured surface

3. Spread a small amount, approximately $\frac{1}{2}$ tsp, mango chutney on each roll

4. Place one shrimp near the bottom of the longest side of dough

5. Roll the shrimp in crescent dough ending with the point on the bottom

6. Make an egg wash beating together 1 large egg and 1 Tbls water

7. Brush each roll with the egg wash and place on baking pan

8. Bake for 15 minutes until golden brown

Serve warm or at room temperature.

Puff Pastry Pizzas
(Makes 24 pieces)

1. Preheat oven to 350 degrees Fahrenheit

2. Put 1 sheet puff pastry dough on floured surface and roll out until very thin, approximately 1/16 inch thick, do the same with a second sheet of puff pastry dough

3. Prick dough all over with fork

4. Cut 24 rounds approximately 3 inches in diameter with pastry cutter or small glass coated with flour

5. Put onto ungreased nonstick baking pan

6. Cut 12 cherry tomatoes in half through the middle and place 1 cherry half, cut side up, on each dough round

7. Put 1 tsp of crumbled feta cheese over tomato

8. Chiffonade 12 medium fresh basil leaves and sprinkle over top

9. Bake for 15 minutes or until golden brown

Serve warm or at room temperature.

Spicy Olives
(Serves 8)

If you can't find olives that have already been pitted, crush olives with a mallet until pit shows and remove pit.

1. Place 1 pound pitted Spanish olives in a large plastic bag

2. In a small bowl, combine:

    a. ½ cup white wine vinegar

    b. ½ cup extra virgin olive oil

    c. 4 Tbls chopped fresh chives

    d. 2 garlic cloves, minced

    e. 2 tsp paprika

    f. 1 tsp black peppercorns

3. Mix well and pour on top of olives

4. Let marinate at room temperature for at least 4 hours or overnight

Drain and serve with decorative toothpicks.

Lychee & Pineapple Skewers
(Makes 24 pieces)

1. Drain 3 14½-oz cans Lychee nuts and 1 large jar or can of pineapple chunks

2. Place one pineapple chunk on a long decorative toothpick, followed by a lychee nut, and then another pineapple chunk

3. Make a chiffonade of fresh mint leaves and sprinkle over the skewers

Cover and refrigerate until serving.

Gin Buck

(Per drink)

1½ oz gin
Juice of ½ medium lemon
Ginger Ale

1. Put gin and lemon juice in cocktail glass filled with ice

2. Top with ginger ale, stir, add straw and garnish with lemon slice

 # Wine

A dry rosé such as a crisp and refreshing French Tavel; or a dry white wine such as a White Bordeaux are Tim's picks to pair with this menu.

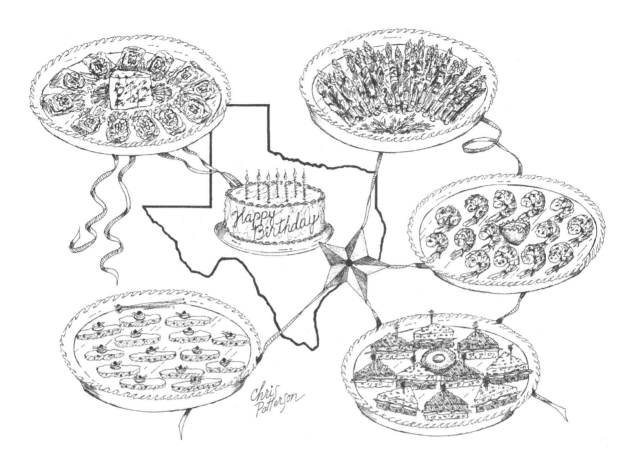

Jim Celebrates a Really Big Birthday

In March of 2010, I celebrated my 25,568th day on earth. Tim and Jeri Richardson (Tim is our wine consultant and Jeri is my food advisor) instigated and graciously hosted the event in their Houston, Texas home. We were joined in the festivities by David and Leslie, our Crystal Lake neighbors who live in Austin, Texas in the winter; Ron, of Ron's Mini Rubens in Menu VII; and many other old time friends. The day started with a luncheon of margaritas and beer at a local bar and then an afternoon of Jeri and me shopping at Central Market for my special cake and the ingredients for the following hors d'œuvres. We had a great time preparing the feast along with "a few" sips of the wine Tim had selected for the party. The affair started at around 7 p.m. and lasted well into my 25,569th day with great memories garnered for future thoughts.

I'm not sure how many bottles of wine we finished but I do know Jeri said that after that party, she had enough corks to finish the beautiful 2' by 5' cork rug she was working on as a gift for me. I found out later that it takes 420 corks to make one rug that size; I didn't ask how far along she was before the party. Some things are better left unknown.

Menu IV

Jim's Birthday Party

(Serves 6 to 8)

Baked Shrimp

Endive with Stilton and Walnuts

Avocado Canapés

Asparagus in Prosciutto

Goat Cheese Stuffed Fingerling Potatoes

Vodka and Tonic Cocktails

I really love this menu, not only because it was served on my birthday with some of my best friends in attendance, but it also included my favorite cheese, Stilton Bleu, and my favorite vegetable, asparagus. All items can be prepared in advance and the menu has all the courses that would be included in a full dinner, especially when served with my birthday cake and lots of wine. The goat cheese fingerling potatoes are courtesy of Jeri Richardson and became a great hit at cocktail parties throughout the summer of 2010. And, what else would be served as the cocktail but Vodka and Tonic, no question, my favorite.

Baked Shrimp

1 pound of raw, peeled and deveined large shrimp (about 18 to 24 pieces), fresh or frozen

2 Tbls olive oil (extra virgin is not needed)

2 Tbls Old Bay Seasoning

1 tsp crushed red pepper (if you want more heat, use a hot chili sauce)

1 medium lemon

Asparagus in Prosciutto

24 medium asparagus spears

1 6-oz package of plain goat cheese

2 to 3 shallots

12 large and very thin slices of prosciutto

Endive with Stilton and Walnuts

3 large Belgian Endives which should give you 24 large separate leaves

12 oz Stilton Bleu cheese

About ½ to ¾ cup real mayonnaise

24 walnut halves

Avocado Canapés

1 loaf dense thinly sliced white bread (Pepperidge Farm)

1 loaf dense thinly sliced wheat bread (Pepperidge Farm)

1 stick unsalted butter

Mayonnaise

24 thin slices Deli roast chicken

3 large avocados

Salt

Decorative toothpicks

Goat Cheese Stuffed Fingerling Potatoes

12 fingerling potatoes (you can substitute Yukon Gold mini potatoes)

5 oz plain goat cheese

2 tsp white truffle or walnut oil

1 tsp Dijon mustard

2 tsp sherry vinegar

2 Tbls extra virgin olive oil

Pink peppercorns (or pimentos) for garnish

1 bunch chives for garnish

White pepper

Salt

Vodka and Tonic

Vodka (Absolut and Blue Ice are my favorites)

Tonic Water (Seagrams is my favorite)

Limes or lemons for garnish

Baked Shrimp
(Makes 18 to 24 pieces)

Be sure to use raw shrimp for this recipe. Fresh shrimp are wonderful but frozen shrimp that have been peeled and deveined (but not pre-cooked) will work just as well and save you a lot of time. Thaw frozen shrimp before using.

1. For each 1 pound of raw, peeled and deveined large shrimp (about 18 to 24), put the following in a bowl and mix together for the marinade:

    a. 2 Tbls olive oil (extra virgin is not needed)

    b. 2 Tbls Old Bay Seasoning

    c. 1 tsp crushed red pepper (if you want more heat, use a hot chili sauce)

    d. Juice from 1 medium lemon

2. Place shrimp in large plastic bag

3. Pour marinade over shrimp and massage shrimp until all are covered

4. Marinate for 1 to 2 hours in refrigerator (but not any longer)

5. Preheat oven to 400 degrees Fahrenheit

6. Place shrimp and marinade in large casserole or baking dish in a single layer, do not overlap

7. Bake for 7 minutes (no longer)

8. Remove immediately from oven

Serve hot, warm, room temperature or cold (do not reheat). These shrimp are very flavorful on their own and do not need to be served with any sauce or dip.

Asparagus in Prosciutto
(Makes 24 pieces)

1. Bring 1 6-oz package of plain goat cheese to room temperature

2. Clean 24 medium asparagus spears

3. Blanch asparagus for 2 minutes then shock by placing in an ice bath to stop the cooking.

4. Finely dice 2 to 3 shallots (you need approximately ½ cup of finely diced shallots)

5. Cut 12 large and very thin slices of prosciutto in half crosswise

6. Take a piece of the prosciutto and spread a very thin coat of the goat cheese on each end

7. Sprinkle a small amount of the shallot on the cheese (both ends)

8. Place 1 asparagus spear on one end of the prosciutto, on top of the cheese, and roll tightly

9. The cheese will hold the prosciutto to the asparagus and keep the package tightly wrapped.

Chill until served (no sauce or dip is necessary). You can prepare this in advance; hours or up to one day, by covering with a damp paper towel and plastic wrap and refrigerating.

Endive with Stilton and Walnuts
(24 pieces)

1. Clean and separate 24 large leaves from 3 Belgian endives (Save the small inner leaves for use in a salad)

2. Put 12 oz of room temperature Stilton Bleu cheese in a food processor

3. Add ½ cup mayonnaise and process until very smooth.

4. It should be of a consistency to pipe thru a piping bag (or a plastic bag with one corner snipped off for piping). If not fluid enough, add more mayonnaise and make sure there are no lumps

5. Place endive leaves on a platter and pipe with cheese mixture

6. Place a walnut half on each

Keep chilled until serving. This can be totally prepared in advance by covering with plastic wrap and refrigerated until served.

Avocado Canapés
(Makes 24 pieces)

1. Trim the crusts from 12 slices of thinly sliced dense white bread and 12 slices thinly sliced dense wheat bread (Pepperidge Farm makes a good thinly sliced dense bread)

2. Spread the white bread with room temperature unsalted butter

3. Spread the wheat bread lightly with mayonnaise

4. Place 2 thin slices of deli roast chicken on the white bread

5. Remove the pit and skin from 3 large avocados

6. Cut avocado into thin slices and place 3 slices on top of chicken

7. Sprinkle each with a very small amount of salt

8. Top with a wheat bread slice and cut diagonally

9. Cover with a damp cloth and chill until serving

10. Toothpicks can be used to secure wedges together

Goat Cheese Stuffed Fingerling Potatoes

(Makes 24 pieces)

1. Prepare the filling by putting the following into a food processor and pulse until smooth:

    a. 5 oz plain goat cheese at room temperature

    b. 2 tsp white truffle oil or walnut oil

    c. ½ tsp salt

    d. ½ tsp pepper (preferably white)

1. Prepare the dressing by whisking together the following in a small bowl:

    a. 1 tsp Dijon mustard

    b. 2 tsp sherry vinegar

    c. 2 Tbls extra virgin olive oil

2. Wash 12 fingerling (or mini Yukon Gold) potatoes, cut the tips off of each end so pieces will sit flat, and then cut in half

3. Use a small melon baller or very small spoon and scoop out the center of each, creating a cavity for the filling

4. Bring a medium size sauce pan of water to a boil and add 2 Tbls salt

5. Put potatoes in boiling water and cook for approx 8 to 10 minutes until just tender (do not overcook)

6. Remove potatoes and put into an ice bath immediately

7. Remove potatoes from bath and drain until dry

8. Put potatoes on a platter, season with salt and pepper and drizzle with the dressing

9. Put the filling in a piping bag or a plastic bag with the corner snipped off for piping

10. Fill the potato cavities completely to just over the top

11. Garnish with 1 pink peppercorn and sprinkle with diced fresh chives. (Pimentos can be substituted for the pink peppercorns)

Chill but bring to room temperature before serving.

Vodka & Tonic

(Per drink)

2½ oz Vodka (I recommend Absolut or Blue Ice Vodka)
4 oz Tonic Water (Seagram's is my favorite)
Lime or lemon wedges

1. Put vodka in small cocktail glass with 3 large ice cubes.

2. Pour tonic on top.

3. Garnish with lime or lemon wedges (optional) and serve.

 **Wine**

Tim recommends a white wine for
this menu. A crisp, elegant and fresh
Sauvignon Blanc would work well as would
a French Sancerre or Muscadet.

Kim "Nose" King Crab

For the last several years Kim Fairchild's daughter, Kate, has brought over forty pounds of King Crab Legs with her when she comes to visit from Chicago; making Crab Night another summer tradition. We cover every flat surface on the porch with newspaper, set out bowls of butter for dipping, tubs of ice for the beer and wine, add a couple of side dishes (usually corn-on-the-cob and Cole slaw), and bring out the heaping platters of steamed crab legs. We always have a big crowd for Crab Night, and now with the deck, we can accommodate even more. I think we had twenty-four people this year. Grab a plate, find a place to sit and dig in; bibs are optional.

Crab Night is great fun and it's spawned another tradition; the smaller brunch we have afterwards to use up any leftovers. We've had a brunch following crab night every year except for one. Last summer, we had about ten pounds of crab legs left over and Kim offered to fix his famous Eggs New Orleans (Eggs Benedict made with crabmeat instead of Canadian bacon) for brunch. He put the crab legs in the back of his car and headed home. When he got home, Kim took Doone, his beautiful collie-mix dog, for their usual walk down to the Frankfort Mineral Springs and back. Yep, the crab legs were completely forgotten; that is until Kim went to stow his recyclables in his car the next afternoon and got a strong reminder.

Menu V

Kim's Party
(Serves 8)

Chicken Liver Mousse

Tuna Tartare

Ham, Gruyère & Dijon Palmiers

Asian Summer Rolls

Parmesan Salmon Cubes

Campari-Orange Cocktails

The recipes in this menu are all courtesy of Kim Fairchild. His chicken liver mousse is one of the great hits of Crystal Lake and is requested by many friends to be prepared for their parties. Kim made the tuna tartare for a dinner party at the home of Larry "Lars" Hilton last summer as an appetizer and has transformed it into an hors d'œuvre for this book. As with many of my friends, his cooking skills never cease to amaze and delight me.

Chicken Liver Mousse

1 pound chicken livers

2½ sticks unsalted butter

2 Tbls cognac

1 large egg

¼ cup heavy cream

¼ tsp allspice

¼ tsp white pepper

1 French baguette or bread of your choice for toasting

Salt

Tuna Tartare

1½ pound sushi grade tuna

1 cup mayonnaise

2 Tbls capers

8 cornichons

1 bunch fresh chives

1 bunch fresh parsley

1 bunch fresh tarragon

1 Tbls whole grain mustard

1 French baguette or bread of your choice for toasting

Ham, Gruyère, & Dijon Palmiers

1 sheet puff pastry dough

2 Tbls Dijon mustard

1 cup freshly grated Gruyère cheese (about 4 oz)

¼ cup freshly grated Parmesan cheese (about 2 oz)

6 oz thinly sliced Prosciutto

Parchment paper

Asian Summer Rolls

24 medium cooked shrimp (2 shrimp per roll)

¼ pound Vermicelli rice noodles

12 8½-inch rounds of rice paper

1 head of iceberg lettuce

¼ cup chopped unsalted peanuts

1 medium red onion

1 clove garlic

14 oz bean sprouts, fresh or canned

1 medium bunch fresh cilantro

1 small bunch fresh mint

Asian Summer Roll Sauce

¼ cup fish sauce

¼ cup rice vinegar

2 limes

1 Tbls sugar

1 Thai chili or 2 Jalapeno peppers

1 medium garlic clove

Parmesan Salmon Cubes

2 pounds thick salmon filets

1 cup freshly grated Parmesan cheese

½ cup flour

¼ tsp seasoned salt

1 tsp paprika

1 large egg

½ cup whole milk

¼ cup (½ stick) unsalted butter

1 garlic clove

Pepper

Campari-Orange Cocktail

Campari

Fresh orange juice

Soda water

Orange slices for garnish

Chicken Liver Mousse
(Serves 12)

1. Preheat oven to 300 degrees Fahrenheit

2. Clean 1 pound of chicken livers and put in food processor

3. Add:

    a. 1 large egg

    b. 2 Tbls cognac

    c. 1 tsp salt

    d. $\frac{1}{4}$ tsp white pepper

    e. $\frac{1}{4}$ tsp allspice

4. Blend for about 30 seconds until well mixed

5. Add $\frac{1}{4}$ cup heavy cream

6. Melt $2\frac{1}{2}$ sticks of unsalted butter and add to chicken mixture

7. Blend for another 30 seconds

8. Pour mixture into a bread loaf pan or 6 ramekins

9. Place pan or ramekins into a bain marie (water bath, a high sided pan with warm water about half way up the sides of the bread loaf pan or ramekins)

10. Bake for 30 minutes or until mixture is firm

11. Remove from oven and bring to room temperature

12. Refrigerate overnight, or at least 8 hours

Serve cold or at room temperature with French bread cut into thin pieces or toast points.

Tuna Tartare

(Serves 8)

1. Finely chop $1\frac{1}{2}$ pounds of sushi grade tuna and place in large bowl

2. Add 1 cup mayonnaise

3. Drain and dice 2 Tbls capers and 8 cornichons and add to mixture

4. Add 2 Tbls each of finely chopped fresh chives, parsley and tarragon

5. Add 1 Tbls whole grain mustard

6. Mix well but leave textured (do not make a paste)

7. Place in decorative bowl that will fit inside another larger bowl

To serve, fill larger bowl with chopped ice and place tartare bowl inside, then place the bowls on a tray with a towel under the bowls to catch any moisture. Serve with sliced and toasted French bread or toast points.

Ham, Gruyère & Dijon Palmiers
(Makes 24 pieces)

1. Thaw 1 sheet of puff pastry dough and roll into a 10X14 inch rectangle (trim edges if necessary)

2. Spread 2 Tbls Dijon mustard over pastry

3. Distribute 1 cup freshly grated Gruyère cheese (about 4 oz) evenly over mustard

4. Distribute ¼ cup freshly grated Parmesan cheese (about 2 oz) evenly over the mustard/Gruyère cheese.

5. Arrange 6 oz of thinly sliced Prosciutto evenly over cheeses

6. Place a sheet of parchment paper over the Prosciutto and using a rolling pin or large straight glass, gently compress the layers

7. Remove the parchment paper and cut the rectangle in half into two 10X7 inch pieces

8. Roll both pieces separately from the 7 inch sides and press edge slightly to keep the rolls together

9. Wrap rolls in plastic wrap and refrigerate for at least 1 hour or overnight

10. Preheat oven to 425 degrees Fahrenheit

11. Remove rolls from refrigerator and plastic wrap and slice each into 12 pieces

12. Use 2 nonstick pans or line baking pans with parchment paper or silpat

13. Place sliced pieces separated on each pan and bake for 10 to 12 minutes until golden brown

If you have a warming tray, these are best served warm, but room temperature is ok.

NOTES

Asian Summer Rolls

(Makes 24 pieces)

1. This will go much easier if you prepare the following ingredients and have them ready in separate bowls (mise en place):

    a. Roughly chop 24 medium cooked shrimp

    b. Roughly chop unsalted peanuts to yield $\frac{1}{4}$ cup

    c. Thinly slice 1 medium red onion

    d. Finely chop 1 clove of garlic

    e. Dice the leaves from 1 medium bunch of fresh cilantro

    f. Dice the leaves from 1 small bunch of fresh mint

    g. 1 cup drained bean sprouts

2. Soak $\frac{1}{4}$ pound Vermicelli rice noodles in cold water for 20 minutes, drain well

3. Using 12, $8\frac{1}{2}$ inch rounds of rice paper; fill large bowl with warm, not hot, water and dip each rice paper round in water for 10 seconds; place damp rice paper rounds, well separated, on work surface

4. Place 1 lettuce leaf on the bottom half of each round

5. Sprinkle equal amounts of chopped peanuts on each round

6. Put a small amount of the sliced red onion on each lower $\frac{1}{3}$ of round

7. Add a tiny bit of the chopped garlic to each lower $\frac{1}{3}$ of round

8. Put an equal amount of bean sprouts on each lower $\frac{1}{3}$ of round

9. Place the chopped shrimp equally on the middle of each round

10. Place equal amounts of rice noodles over shrimp

11. Sprinkle cilantro and mint over each round

12. Start rolling each round from filled bottom

13. As soon as you have made one turn, where rice paper roll wraps under filling, fold in the side edge of each round and continue rolling into a cylinder

14. The final edge should stick, if not, dampen with a bit of water and press lightly

15. Place cylinders in flat casserole dish, cover with a damp paper towel then plastic wrap

16. Refrigerate until ready to serve

Sauce for serving:

1. Mix the following ingredients together in a medium bowl until sugar dissolves:

    a. $\frac{1}{4}$ cup fish sauce

    b. $\frac{1}{4}$ cup rice vinegar

    c. 3 Tbls lime juice

    d. 1 Tbls sugar

    e. 1 Thai chili or 2 jalapenos peppers, stemmed and seeded, finely diced

    f. 1 medium garlic clove, finely diced

2. Refrigerate until ready to serve

To serve, cut each cylinder thru the center on the diagonal, making 24 pieces. Place on decorative platter with the sauce in the middle with a small spoon.

Menu V

NOTES

Parmesan Salmon Cubes

(Makes about 24 pieces)

1. Preheat oven to 350 degrees Fahrenheit

2. Cut 2 pounds of thick salmon filets into about $1\frac{1}{2}$ inch cubes

3. In a medium bowl, mix:

    a. 1 cup freshly grated Parmesan cheese

    b. $\frac{1}{2}$ cup flour

    c. $\frac{1}{4}$ tsp seasoned salt

    d. $\frac{1}{2}$ tsp freshly ground black pepper

    e. 1 tsp paprika

4. In another bowl, beat 1 large egg well and add $\frac{1}{2}$ cup milk

5. Dip salmon cubes first into egg mixture and then into Parmesan mixture

6. Place cubes on a lightly greased baking pan

7. Over medium low heat, melt $\frac{1}{4}$ cup ($\frac{1}{2}$ stick) unsalted butter. Add 1 minced clove of garlic and sauté lightly (do not brown)

8. Drizzle the butter/garlic over the salmon cubes and bake for 30 minutes until lightly browned and salmon flakes

Best served warm, but room temperature is ok.

50

Campari-Orange

(Per drink)

2 oz Campari
1 oz fresh orange juice
4 oz soda water
Orange slices

1. Put 2 oz of Campari and 1 oz of fresh orange juice in a tall glass with ice

2. Top with 4 oz of soda water and stir

3. Garnish with an orange slice (optional)

 # Wine

Tim recommends a lighter red wine such as the less acidic Cabernet Franc, either domestic or from the Loire Valley, for this menu. Another possible lighter red wine is a drier Pinot Noir. The complex flavors and soft, velvety texture of the Pinot Noir would pair well with all the hors d'œuvres here.

Guess Who's Coming to Dinner

Last summer Bob Weber brought his grandson Dugan to one of our dinners on the porch. I was a little concerned about how Dugan, a single 26 year old vegetarian with what can most kindly be described as unusual eating habits, would fare at dinner. Dugan, who is also a writer, sent me the following story about his experience.

"There's never been a shortage of people concerned about my diet or the bohemian lifestyle I stumbled into leading. Plates and cups are rarely needed; I shift from one bag of potato chips to another, eating behavior that Grandpa Bob has described as "grazing". Add genetic pickiness to the equation, it means that at 26 I have an unsophisticated palate and no working knowledge of cuisines. But in my defense, the absence of a dish trail from the bedroom to the sink has always made me a popular roommate.

A Michigan visit, however, was an awesome departure from the routine. Jim not only cooked some great meals but took into consideration the fact that I'm a vegetarian. From what I can tell, great skill, foresight and a semblance of casualness is served with each night's preparation; and, through the charcoal smoke and steam comes a steady stream of jokes - usually at someone's expense. The food was complimented by scenery. I could literally feel Michigan's pride while seated on the porch overlooking the lake ready to dine with pals. I felt such an urge to say something meaningful, of course, I was awed, so I also felt an urge to say nothing at all. I yield the floor to my Grandpa, who sums it up thusly: "We live well, don't we?""

Menu VI

Live Well
(Serves 8)

Easy Deviled Eggs

Dates Stuffed with Cream Cheese and Walnuts

Puff Pastry with Caviar

Stuffed Cucumbers with Crabmeat

Sausage & Pepper Kabobs

Margarita Cocktails

This is another almost meatless menu which could become meatless by substituting cherry tomatoes for the sausage in the kabobs. The combination of flavors between the creamy deviled eggs, the salty caviar and the spicy sausage will give every palate a treat to remember. The dates rolled in sugar are a perfect finish to a complete hors d'œuvre party.

Easy Deviled Eggs

12 large eggs

4 Tbls mayonnaise

2 tsp Dijon mustard

½ tsp onion powder

½ tsp celery salt

¼ tsp white pepper

Capers, caviar, anchovies, pimentos, or whatever for topping of deviled eggs

Salt

Stuffed Dates

1 8-oz box whole pitted dates

1 3-oz package cream cheese

¼ cup powdered sugar

1 Tbls heavy cream

¼ cup chopped walnuts (if you can find powdered walnuts, all the better)

Puff Pastry with Cavier

1 sheet puff pastry dough

½ cup plain sour cream

2 oz caviar (of your choice)

1 bunch fresh chives

1 large egg

Cucumbers Stuffed with Crabmeat

2 English cucumbers

8 oz lump crabmeat

4 Tbls mayonnaise

1 Tbls ketchup

1 bunch fresh tarragon

2 tsp Dijon mustard

4 Tbls extra virgin olive oil

4 tsp red wine vinegar

Salt and pepper

Sausage & Pepper Kabobs

3 bratwurst (flavor of your choice, I like jalapeno myself)

3 yellow or red bell peppers

1 can beer (of your choice, don't forget to have 1 extra for the chef)

2 Tbls extra virgin olive oil

Salt and pepper

Long decorative toothpicks

Margarita

Tequila

Triple Sec

Fresh limes

Salt

Easy Deviled Eggs
(Makes 24 pieces)

1. Hard boil 12 large eggs, peel, and cut in half lengthwise (See page 98 for the best way to hard boil eggs.)

2. Put egg yolks in a bowl; using a fork, mash until smooth

3. Add 4 Tbls mayonnaise and 2 tsp Dijon mustard and mix

4. Add: $\frac{1}{2}$ tsp onion powder, $\frac{1}{2}$ tsp celery salt, $\frac{1}{2}$ tsp of salt, and $\frac{1}{4}$ tsp white pepper

5. Mix until smooth and put into small re-sealable plastic bag

6. Cut a small piece off one corner of the bag and squeeze mixture into the egg halves

7. Top with your favorite garnish, I recommend either capers, caviar, anchovies, or pimentos

Keep refrigerated until ready to serve.

Stuffed Dates
(Makes 24 pieces)

1. Finely grind $\frac{1}{4}$ cup chopped walnuts in a coffee or spice grinder

2. Place the following in a food processor and pulse until smooth:
   a. 3 oz of room temperature cream cheese
   b. $\frac{1}{4}$ cup powdered sugar
   c. 1 Tbls cream
   d. The finely ground walnuts

3. Put mixture in a piping bag with medium point or a plastic bag with corner cut off

4. Place 24 dates on a platter and make a slit in the top of each

5. Pipe cream cheese mixture into each date

Cover and refrigerate until serving. You can prepare this recipe the night before and, if desired, roll the filled dates in more powdered sugar just before serving for a sweeter dessert.

NOTES

Puff Pastry with Caviar
(Makes 24 to 30 pieces)

1. Preheat oven to 400 degrees Fahrenheit

2. Dice 1 bunch of fresh chives and set aside

3. Unroll 1 thawed puff pastry sheet onto lightly floured surface

4. Cut sheet into 12 to 15 shapes, using any small cookie cutter or small glass

5. Place on a lightly greased nonstick baking pan or use parchment paper or silpat

6. Make an egg wash by beating 1 large egg with 1 Tbls water

7. Brush each pastry with egg wash

8. Bake for 12 to 15 minutes, until puffed and golden brown

9. Cool and then split horizontally

10. Place 1 scant tsp sour cream on each cooled pastry

11. Top each with a small amount of caviar, you will need about 2 oz of caviar for entire recipe

12. Sprinkle each with diced chives

Serve at room temperature within 2 hours of making or pastry will become soggy.

Cucumbers Stuffed with Crabmeat
(Makes about 24 pieces)

1. Rinse and cut the ends off 2 English cucumbers (you do not need to peel English cucumbers)

2. Slice each cucumber into about 12 equal pieces, about 1 inch plus thick each

3. Scoop out the center of each piece with a small melon baller without going all the way thru

4. Bring a large pot of water to a boil and add 1 heaping Tbls salt

5. Drop cucumber pieces into boiling water for 1 minute

6. Drain and put immediately into an ice bath

7. Remove when cooled and drain on paper towels or clean cloth

8. Make vinaigrette by mixing together the following:

    a. 4 Tbls extra virgin olive oil

    b. 4 tsp red wine vinegar

    c. 2 tsp Dijon mustard

    d. 1 tsp salt

    e. $\frac{1}{2}$ tsp freshly ground pepper

9. Put cucumber pieces on large tray and sprinkle with the vinaigrette

10. Make the crab filling by lightly mixing together the following

    a. 8 oz lump crabmeat checked for any shells and broken into small pieces

    b. 4 Tbls mayonnaise

    c. 1 Tbls ketchup

    d. 2 Tbls chopped fresh tarragon

11. Spoon crabmeat filling into cucumber slices

Cover and chill until serving. This can be served chilled or at room temperature.

Sausage & Pepper Kabobs
(Makes 24 to 30 pieces)

1. Put 3 bratwurst (any flavor, I like Jalapeno) and 1 can of beer in a medium pot and bring to low boil

2. Reduce heat and simmer for 20 to 30 minutes until firm

3. Remove and bring to room temperature

4. Clean and cut 3 yellow (or 3 red) peppers into 16 to 20 small pieces each (total of 48 to 60 pieces)

5. Put pepper pieces into pot with hot beer for 2 minutes

6. Remove pepper pieces, drain, put in bowl and add:

    a. 2 Tbls extra virgin olive oil

    b. ½ tsp salt

    c. ¼ tsp freshly ground black pepper

7. Mix and let sit for 10 minutes until cool

8. Slice bratwurst in ½ to ¾ inch pieces, about 8 to 10 per sausage

9. Assemble kabobs by placing one piece of pepper on a long decorative toothpick followed by one piece of the bratwurst and then another piece of pepper

This can be done 1 day in advance and kept refrigerated until serving. Serve at room temperature.

Margarita

(Per drink)

1½ oz Tequila
½ oz triple sec
1 oz fresh lime juice
Salt

1. Dip the rim of a cocktail glass into the squeezed lime juice and then into the salt.

2. Put Tequila, triple sec, lime juice and ice in a shaker.

3. Shake well and strain into salt rimmed glass with or without ice.

 # Wine

Tim recommends a nice sparkling white wine for this menu. Champagne, Italian Prosecco, or a generally less expensive Spanish Cava would all work beautifully.

How Jim and Nan Celebrate the Fourth of July

The Fourth of July Holiday is a huge event in Frankfort. This is when every cottage is full of two, three, and sometimes even four generations of family. Nan and I start celebrating on July 3 with Jim Beck's annual pitch-in. Jim hasn't sent out invitations to his July 3rd party in years, people just come and even bring their houseguests with them. It's always fun to see who shows up.

On July 4th we like to go into Frankfort and see the parade. I've been going to the parade all my life and it hasn't changed much over the years. After the parade and some unabashed flag waving, I head back to Sunny Shores to finish preparations for our cookout. We have anywhere from 10 to 20 people over for an all-American meal of grilled white fish, corn on the cob, fresh tomato salad, and cherry pie before heading to Patsy and Bill Beck's (no relation to Jim Beck) for their annual lawn party. The Becks' home sits on the Frankfort Beach, overlooking the Frankfort Breakwater and is the perfect spot for watching the fireworks. We "ooh" and "aah" with the rest of the crowd on the beach until the grand finale of red, white, and blue explosions. We head home about midnight, exhausted but so happy and grateful to be in this place and of this time.

I took the meatballs in wine sauce from the next menu to Jim Beck's July 3rd party last year and it was one of the first dishes to disappear.

Menu VII

Holiday Fireworks
(Serves 8)

Meatballs in Wine Sauce

Ron's Mini Rubens

Garlic Roasted Brussels Sprouts

Cajun Shrimp Bruschetta

Chocolate Covered Strawberries

Mojito Cocktails

This menu would work as a full Fourth of July dinner as well as a cocktail party. All items can be made ahead of time, allowing you to participate in all the day's activities and attend all the other parties without feeling stressed. Ron's mini Rubens were put together and tested many times on my visit to his new home in The Garden District of New Orleans this last November.

Shopping List

Meatballs in Wine Sauce

1 pound ground beef (you can substitute ground turkey)

1 large egg

2 Tbls heavy cream

½ cup bread crumbs (plain, not seasoned)

1 small onion

½ tsp Worcestershire sauce

1 jar grape jelly, 6 to 8 oz

1 bottle Burgundy wine (you can substitute a dry red wine of your choice, e.g. Chianti works well)

1 14-oz can low sodium beef broth

2 Tbls corn starch

Salt and pepper

Decorative toothpicks

Ron's Mini Rubens

1 loaf Pepperidge Farm thin sliced dense rye bread

24 large thin slices deli corned beef (about ½ pound)

1 small jar Thousand Island dressing

1 small can or bag sauerkraut

6 oz sliced Swiss cheese

Garlic Roasted Brussels Sprouts

24 small Brussels sprouts

6 garlic cloves

3 Tbls extra virgin olive oil

Salt and pepper

Decorative toothpicks

Cajun Shrimp Bruschetta

48 medium (25-35 pieces per pound) uncooked shrimp

1 French baguette

1 stick unsalted butter

1 to 2 bunches (about 8) green onions

4 cloves garlic

1 oz brandy or cognac

Worcestershire sauce

¼ tsp cayenne pepper

1 bunch parsley

Salt

Chocolate Covered Strawberries

24 large fresh strawberries that still have the stems attached

2 packages of dipping chocolate, either dark or semi-sweet (if you cannot find dipping chocolate, use 2, 3½-oz bars of good quality dark or semi-sweet chocolate and 2 Tbls heavy cream)

Mojito Cocktails

Light rum

Limes

Sugar

Mint sprigs

Soda water

Meatballs in Wine Sauce

(Makes about 24 pieces)

You could use frozen meatballs for this recipe and just make the sauce, but the meatballs are so easy to make and homemade is always better.

1. Preheat oven to 350 degrees Fahrenheit

2. In a large bowl beat one large egg, add the following and mix well:

   a. 2 Tbls heavy cream

   b. ½ cup plain bread crumbs

   c. 1 small minced onion

   d. ½ tsp Worcestershire Sauce

   e. ½ tsp salt and ¼ tsp pepper

3. Add 1 pound ground beef (you can substitute ground turkey) in pieces and mix with your clean hands

4. Form into 1 inch balls and put in a nonstick baking pan

5. Bake for 25 to 30 minutes and check that center is done by cutting one in half

You can refrigerate overnight or freeze for future use at this point.

6. Make the sauce by:

   a. Combining one bottle Burgundy wine with 1 6-oz to 8-oz jar of grape jelly, and 1 14-oz can low sodium beef broth in a large sauce pan.

   b. Bring to a low boil

   c. Put 2 Tbls corn starch in a small bowl, add 2 Tbls water and mix well

   d. Slowly add the corn starch mixture to the wine sauce and return to a low boil

   e. Turn heat to low and simmer for 30 minutes until thick

7. Put room temperature or warm meatballs in a crock pot or chafing dish and add wine sauce

Keep on low temperature and serve with decorative toothpicks. You can do this 4 or 5 hours in advance and keep warm until serving.

Ron's Mini Rubens

(Makes 32 pieces)

1. Put 1 small can or bag of sauerkraut into colander and drain well

2. Take 8 slices of thinly sliced dense rye bread and toast until crisp (leave the crusts on)

3. Spread each slice lightly with Thousand Island dressing, about 1 scant tsp each

4. Put 3 thin slices of deli corned beef on each piece, covering the entire surface

5. Put a scant Tbls of sauerkraut on each and spread evenly over slice

6. Place one slice of Swiss cheese on each

You can make to this point, cover and let stand until ready to broil (2 to 3 hours is ok).

7. Preheat broiler and broil about 4 inches from flame until bubbly, about 3 to 4 minutes

8. Cool and cut slices into 4 square pieces

These are best served warm with a warming tray, but room temperature is ok.

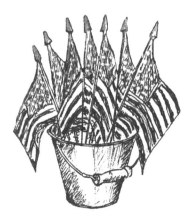

Garlic Roasted Brussels Sprouts
(Makes 24 pieces)

1. Cut base off of 24 small Brussels sprouts and remove any damaged leaves, making all the sprouts close to the same size

2. Cut a small X into the top of each sprout using a sharp paring knife

3. Put 2 Tbls salt into large bowl and add cold water

4. Put Brussels sprouts into bowl, sprouts should be covered with the salt water

5. Let stand at room temperature for at least 2 hours

6. Mince 6 garlic cloves

7. Preheat oven to 400 degrees Fahrenheit

8. Drain water from bowl containing Brussels sprouts, do not rinse

9. Put 3 Tbls extra virgin olive oil over Brussels sprouts and toss to cover

10. Add the minced garlic

11. Add 1 tsp salt and ½ tsp pepper and toss again

12. Put into oven proof casserole in one layer and bake for 20 to 30 minutes until soft and golden brown.

13. Let cool to room temperature.

Serve with long decorative toothpicks or refrigerate until ready to serve (one or two days is ok), return to room temperature to serve.

Cajun Shrimp Bruschetta
(Makes 24 pieces)

1. Clean and devein 48 medium (25-35 pieces per pound) uncooked shrimp, removing all shells and tail

2. Melt one stick unsalted butter in large skillet over medium heat

3. Add $\frac{1}{2}$ cup chopped green onions and 1 tsp diced garlic and cook for 3 to 4 minutes until tender

4. Add the shrimp and cook for about 5 minutes until they turn pink, do not overcook, remove the shrimp from skillet

5. Add 1 oz brandy (or cognac), 2 dashes Worcestershire sauce, $\frac{1}{2}$ tsp salt and $\frac{1}{4}$ tsp cayenne pepper

6. Cook for another 3 to 4 minutes to reduce sauce

7. Remove skillet from heat, add shrimp, stir and cool to room temperature.

8. Cut 1 French baguette into 24 thin slices and toast lightly

9. Place two shrimp plus a little reduced sauce on each slice and garnish with chopped fresh parsley

This can be done until assembly point and kept refrigerated overnight.
Serve warm or at room temperature.

Chocolate Covered Strawberries
(Makes 24 pieces)

1. Rinse 24 large fresh strawberries to remove any sand; leave green leafy part and stem on the berry

2. Heat 2 packages of dipping chocolate according to package directions (if you cannot find dipping chocolate, breakup 2 $3\frac{1}{2}$-oz bars of a good quality dark or semi-sweet chocolate in a double boiler and heat with 2 Tbls heavy cream until melted and smooth)

3. Put melted chocolate in deep bowl and holding strawberry by stem, dip each strawberry to just below the stem, let excess chocolate drip back into bowl

4. Place on waxed paper sheets to cool

You can refrigerate for 1 to 2 days before serving cold or at room temperature.

Mojito Cocktails

(Per drink)

2 oz light rum
1 oz fresh lime juice
2 tsp sugar
2 mint leaves
2 oz soda water

1. Put sugar, 1 mint leaf, and splash of soda in a shaker

2. Muddle with pestle or long wooden spoon

3. Add rum and ice and shake well

4. Strain over cracked ice in cocktail glass and top with the other mint leaf

 # Wine

Tim recommends a full bodied, deep red wine such as a Shiraz, Carmenere, or Nero d'Avola for this menu. The strong and somewhat fruity flavors of the wines will stand up to these hearty dishes.

If I Had a Beach Party

When I was a college student, I spent my summers working at the old Crystal Beach Resort. It didn't pay much, about $35 a week, but more importantly, it was my excuse to my parents for staying at the lake all summer. This was not uncommon. The whole county was filled with college students waiting tables, dishing out ice cream, and working in the local retail stores and resorts. After work, beach parties were the mainstay of our social lives. All we needed was a large fire on a Lake Michigan beach, the moon and millions of stars shimmering off the lake, some cheap wine and beer, someone playing "If I Had a Hammer" on their guitar, and miles of sand dunes between us and our parents or any local authorities.

Last summer a group of us decided we should pay homage and have an old fashion beach party except with better food and drinks. We decided to have it on the beach by Point Betsie Lighthouse on Lake Michigan, a favorite location when we were kids. Well, lugging coolers, blankets, and wood across the sand just to try and stay warm by a fire somehow doesn't hold the same appeal at this age as it did at 18. We decided to have a party on the deck instead.

Menu VIII

~~Beach~~ Deck Party
(Serves 8)

Roasted Garlic Bruschetta

Crabmeat Strudel

Steak Carpaccio Bruschetta

Mini Cocktail Sandwiches

Cookies & Cream

A Day at the Beach Cocktail

This menu encompasses not only items you could take to the beach like the mini cocktail sandwiches, the roasted garlic bruschetta and the cookies & cream, but two more elegant dishes, the crabmeat strudel and the steak Carpaccio which lend themselves to a more sophisticated occasion. With a little extra planning and effort even these could go to the beach and WOW your guests.

Roasted Garlic Bruschetta

1 French baguette

4 heads of garlic

Extra virgin olive oil, about 2½ Tbls

1 bunch of fresh basil

Salt and pepper

Crabmeat Strudel

2 packages filo (phyllo) dough

2 pounds lump crabmeat

2 sticks unsalted butter

6 green onions

4 cloves garlic

2 limes

1 bunch parsley

2 tsp curry powder

1 cup unflavored bread crumbs

Steak Carpaccio Bruschetta

1 12-oz piece prime beef tenderloin

2 Tbls extra virgin olive oil

1 Tbls coarse salt

2 cups lightly packed arugula or fresh baby spinach

2 oz freshly shaved Parmesan cheese

2 Tbls fresh lemon juice

1 French baguette

Pepper

Mini Cocktail Sandwiches

1 loaf cocktail rye bread

1 stick unsalted butter

12 thin slices smoked turkey

12 thin slices rare roast beef

Dijon mustard (about 2 Tbls)

Mayonnaise (about 2 Tbls)

1 package arugula or baby spinach

Decorative toothpicks (optional)

Cookies & Cream

24 Shortbread cookies

1 8-oz package mascarpone cheese

12 large strawberries

1 bunch fresh mint

A Day at the Beach Cocktail

Captain Morgan Rum

Amaretto

Fresh orange juice

Grenadine

Strawberries for garnish

Roasted Garlic Bruschetta
(Makes 24 pieces)

1. Preheat oven to 400 degrees Fahrenheit

2. Take outer layers of husks from 4 garlic heads, leaving cloves intact

3. Cut about $\frac{1}{4}$ inch off the top of the garlic head (the stem end is the bottom)

4. Place in small baking dish, separated, not stacked, stem side down

5. Sprinkle about 2 Tbls olive oil over top of heads

6. Bake for 20 to 30 minutes until soft and mushy

7. Remove and cool to room temperature

8. Squeeze garlic pulp from heads, this could be quite messy on your hands, into bowl

9. Pour any remaining olive oil from pan into bowl

10. Add 1 tsp olive oil and salt and pepper to taste

11. Lightly mash with a fork

You can prepare up to this point one or two days ahead and refrigerate, but bring to room temperature before continuing

12. Cut 1 French baguette into 24 thin slices and lightly toast

13. Spread each toast slice with garlic pulp

14. Chiffonade 1 bunch of fresh basil and place some on each garlic toast

Serve at room temperature on a decorative tray.

Crabmeat Strudel

(Makes about 24 pieces)

1. Thaw 2 packages filo (phyllo) dough

2. Preheat oven to 400 degrees Fahrenheit

3. Clean and dice 6 green onions and 4 garlic cloves

4. Melt 4 Tbls unsalted butter in a skillet over medium high heat

5. Add onions and garlic and sauté until tender but not browned

6. Add 2 tsp curry powder and mix well

7. Check 2 pounds lump crabmeat for shells and chop into small pieces, put in a large bowl, add and mix lightly:

    a. juice of 2 limes

    b. 8 Tbls chopped parsley

    c. the sautéed onions and garlic

8. Melt 8 Tbls unsalted butter in a small bowl or pan

9. Unwrap the thawed filo dough and place one layer of dough on a lightly floured surface

10. Brush with the melted butter and sprinkle lightly with the unflavored bread crumbs

11. Put a second layer of filo on top and repeat with melted butter and bread crumbs

12. Repeat with 2 more layers of filo dough, each with melted butter and bread crumbs

13. Place the crabmeat filling evenly down one edge of the Filo dough

14. Roll tightly into a cylinder

15. Place on a nonstick baking pan or use a pan lined with parchment paper or silpat, seam side down

16. Lightly score the cylinder into approximately $1\frac{1}{2}$ inch long pieces and brush with remaining melted butter

17. Bake for 15 to 20 minutes until golden brown

Let cool to room temperature. Slice through score marks and serve on a decorative platter.

Steak Carpaccio Bruschetta

(Makes 24 pieces)

1. Tie 1, 12-oz prime beef tenderloin with kitchen twine to help maintain its shape

2. Freeze tied beef until totally frozen

3. Heat 1 Tbls olive oil in a large heavy skillet over high heat

4. Rub frozen meat with 1 Tbls coarse salt and ½ Tbls freshly ground black pepper on all sides

5. Put beef in the skillet and sear on all sides, about 4 minutes in total

6. Refreeze beef until it is almost totally frozen, about 1 hour

7. Using a very sharp carving knife, slice beef as thinly as possible

8. Put 2 cups lightly packed arugula (or baby spinach) in a bowl and dress with 1 Tbls olive oil and 2 Tbls freshly squeezed lemon juice, sprinkle with salt and pepper

9. Cut 1 French baguette into 24 thin slices and lightly toast

10. Place a few pieces of arugula (or spinach) on each toast piece

11. Place a small amount of sliced beef on each and top with shaved Parmesan

You can prepare the beef through slicing (step #7) ahead of time and keep refrigerated until final assembly.

Place on decorative platter and serve at room temperature.

Mini Cocktail Sandwiches

(Makes 24 pieces)

You will need 12 thin slices of smoked turkey and 12 thin slices of rare roast beef for this dish. You can substitute any sliced meat that you prefer but I would suggest these two choices.

1. Lightly spread 48 slices of cocktail rye bread with room temperature unsalted butter

2. Take 12 slices of the bread and spread lightly with Dijon mustard

3. Add 1 slice of roast beef to each of the 12 slices with the Dijon mustard, top with arugula or spinach and cover with a slice of the plain buttered rye

4. Take 12 slices of rye and spread lightly with mayonnaise

5. Add 1 slice of smoked turkey to each, top with arugula or spinach and cover with another slice of buttered rye

6. Place in a container, cover with a damp paper towel and plastic wrap and keep cool until serving at room temperature

Serve as is or put a decorative toothpick in each sandwich.

Cookies & Cream

(Makes 24 pieces)

1. Bring 1 8-oz package mascarpone cheese to room temperature

2. Spread mascarpone cheese lightly on 24 shortbread cookies

3. Clean, remove stems and cut 12 large strawberries in half

4. Put strawberry slices on top of the cheese spread shortbread cookies

5. Chiffonade fresh mint and put some on each strawberry

Chill, but bring to room temperature before serving.

A Day
at the Beach

(Per drink)

1 oz Captain Morgan Rum
$\frac{1}{2}$ oz amaretto
4 oz fresh orange juice
$\frac{1}{2}$ oz grenadine

1. Put all ingredients but the grenadine in a
    shaker with ice and mix well.

2. Strain into a tall glass with ice

3. Add grenadine and top with a strawberry

 # Wine

Tim recommends a Tuscan red wine with this
menu such as a strong and bold Chianti or a
somewhat softer Montepulciano. The rich
aromas and viscosity of an American Barbera
or a California Sangiovese would also
go with these well-seasoned foods.

Bob and Betsie Host a Party
and Do a Good Deed

Every summer my lifelong Crystal Lake friend, Betsie Hosick, and her companion Bob Weber, host an afternoon cookout in front of their lovely home overlooking Lake Michigan. The party is timed to coincide with the famous sailboat race from Chicago to Mackinac Island and, weather permitting, we all have a great time watching the boats sail by on their way around the Manitou Islands and on to Mackinac. Betsie and Bob provide the hamburgers, hot dogs, brats, and chicken for grilling and several guests bring dishes to add to the bounty. Last year there was an exceptional amount of food. When Betsie and Bob saw the amount of leftovers, they decided to take some "care packages" over to our friend and my business partner, Marjorie Elliott, who had a house full of family members arriving that day for a week-long stay. Bob and Betsie know that Marjorie is, well . . .let's just say, not much of a cook and would appreciate having the prepared food. Later, Marjorie admitted that her family was more than a little surprised by the cheese trays, hors d'œuvres, snacks, and desserts they were served all week. I wonder if they are beginning to think she can cook?

The next menu includes a recipe for marinated vegetables. It's a great hors d'œuvre that travels well and is perfect when you need to take something to an afternoon party.

Menu IX

Good in Deed
(Serves 8)

Cubed Cheese Tray

Marinated Vegetables

Three Sausages with Pickled Garlic

Tuna Croquettes

Portobello Bruschetta with Stilton Butter

Long Island Iced Tea Cocktails

This menu has two of the easiest and quickest recipes to prepare and if done with quality ingredients and a little care when putting together the presentation, they will be a great hit. The tuna croquettes and the portobello bruschettas are the most time consuming, so if you want a quick easy party, substitute with possibly the mini cocktail sandwiches from Menu VIII and a dessert like the chocolate strawberries from Menu VII.

Cubed Cheese Tray

12 oz extra sharp Cheddar cheese

12 oz smoked Gouda

12 oz Swiss cheese

1 package of cherry tomatoes

Lettuce leaves for covering the serving platter

Decorative toothpicks

Marinated Vegetables

1 jar marinated green asparagus

1 jar marinated white asparagus

1 medium can pitted black olives

1 medium can stuffed green olives (stuffing of your choice)

1 can marinated artichoke hearts

1 jar marinated mixed vegetables, either mild or hot

1 jar marinated spicy peppers

Lettuce or spinach leaves to cover serving plate

Decorative toothpicks

Three Sausages with Pickled Garlic

1 sweet Italian sausage

1 mild Italian sausage

1 hot Italian sausage

1 bottle beer

1 jar pickled garlic

1 head iceberg lettuce

1 Tbls olive oil (does not need to be extra virgin)

Decorative toothpicks

Tuna Croquettes

1 $6\frac{1}{2}$-oz can or package tuna

2 large eggs

2 large Idaho or Yukon Gold potatoes

1 small jar pimentos

1 small yellow onion

Pinch of cayenne pepper

1 cup dry unflavored bread crumbs

Oil for deep frying

Salt and pepper

Decorative toothpicks

Optional Sauce:

1 cup mayonnaise

1 Tbls Dijon mustard

Portobello Bruschetta with Stilton Butter

1 French baguette

24 baby portobello mushrooms

$\frac{1}{2}$ cup olive oil (extra virgin not necessary)

5 Tbls balsamic vinegar

6 large garlic cloves

1 bunch fresh thyme

4 oz Stilton Bleu cheese

4 oz unsalted butter

Long Island Iced Tea Cocktails

Vodka

Tequila

Rum

Gin

Triple sec

Coca Cola (not diet)

Lemon slices for garnish (optional)

Cubed Cheese Tray
(Serves 8)

Do not buy already cubed cheese unless you can personally taste each cheese before purchase.

1. Cut the following cheeses into bite size pieces:
    a. 12 oz extra sharp Cheddar
    b. 12 oz smoked Gouda
    c. 12 oz Swiss
2. Rinse and dry 1 package cherry tomatoes
3. Decorate a large platter with several leaves of lettuce
4. Place tomatoes in the middle with the cheeses around the edge

Chill until serving at room temperature with decorative toothpicks.

Marinated Vegetables
(Serves 8)

You can use any marinated vegetable of your choice for this hors d'œuvre. I like the following combination and I think it makes for a very elegant dish and an attractive display on a platter.

1. Take a large platter, cover with lettuce or spinach leaves, and arrange the following vegetables on top with a bowl of decorative toothpicks in the middle.
    a. 1 jar drained marinated green asparagus
    b. 1 jar drained marinated white asparagus
    c. 1 can drained pitted black olives
    d. 1 can drained stuffed green olives (stuffing of your choice)
    e. 1 can drained marinated artichoke hearts
    f. 1 jar drained marinated mixed vegetables
    g. 1 jar drained marinated spicy peppers

You could also use a platter that has partitions, just don't forget to find a place for the decorative toothpicks and a small side dish for used toothpicks.

Three Sausages with Pickled Garlic
(Makes about 30 pieces)

1. Bring 1 sweet Italian sausage, 1 mild Italian sausage, and 1 hot Italian sausage to room temperature

2. Put one bottle of beer and the 3 sausages into a large pot

3. Bring to a low boil and cook for 15 to 20 minutes, until sausages are firm

4. Remove from pot and bring to room temperature

5. Slice sausages into about 10 slices each about $\frac{1}{2}$ to $\frac{3}{4}$ inches thick

6. Preheat a large skillet on medium high and add 1 Tbls olive oil

7. Lightly brown sausage pieces on each side and drain on paper towels

8. Shred one head of iceberg lettuce onto a large platter

9. Arrange sausage slices around platter in a spiral pattern starting at center, overlapping slightly

10. Drain one small jar of pickled garlic and scatter over sausages

Serve with long decorative toothpicks (don't forget a small bowl for used picks).

Tuna Croquettes

(Makes about 24 pieces)

1. Boil 2 large Idaho or Yukon Gold potatoes for 20 minutes until tender; drain, peel, mash, and set aside.

2. In a large bowl, beat 1 large egg until frothy

3. Add:
   a. 1 6½-oz can (packed in oil or water) flaked tuna
   b. 1 cup mashed potatoes,
   c. 1 Tbls chopped pimentos,
   d. 1 Tbls minced yellow onion,
   e. Pinch of cayenne pepper
   f. ¼ tsp salt
   g. Pinch of freshly ground black pepper

4. Mix well and then add enough unflavored bread crumbs to bind mixture, about ¼ to ½ cups

5. Roll the mixture into balls about the size of quarters or large marbles

6. Put 1 large egg into a shallow dish and beat well

7. Put ½ to ¾ cups bread crumbs into another shallow dish

8. Roll each tuna ball in the egg and then the bread crumbs

9. Place tuna balls on a platter lined with wax paper and chill for at least 1 hour

10. Fry croquettes in hot oil (375 degrees Fahrenheit) for 3 to 4 minutes until golden brown

11. Drain on paper towels

A sauce is not necessary, but you could serve a mayonnaise/mustard sauce on the side.

12. Mayonnaise/mustard sauce: combine 1 cup mayonnaise with 1 Tbls Dijon mustard and mix well.

Serve croquettes warm or at room temperature in a bowl with long decorative toothpicks and a separate bowl for the discarded picks.

Portobello Bruschetta
with Stilton Butter

(Makes 24 pieces)

1. Cut the stems of 24 baby portobello mushrooms even with the caps and clean with damp cloth

2. Combine ½ cup olive oil with 5 Tbls balsamic vinegar and add:

   a. 6 large garlic cloves, minced

   b. 2 Tbls chopped fresh thyme

3. Put the mushrooms in a large plastic bag and pour the marinade over mushrooms

4. Seal bag and massage lightly to ensure good mixture

5. Marinate at room temperature for at least 1 hour, 2 hours maximum

6. Preheat broiler

7. Place drained mushrooms on a baking sheet and broil on each side for 2 to 3 minutes, about 4 inches below broiler, until tender

8. Remove and let cool to room temperature

9. Make the Stilton butter by mixing 4 oz of room temperature Stilton Bleu cheese and 4 oz room temperature unsalted butter until smooth

You can do this entire recipe to this point and keep refrigerated overnight, but take out and bring to room temperature before finishing.

10. Cut 1 French baguette into 24 thin slices and toast lightly

11. Coat each toasted slice with a small amount of the Stilton butter

12. Place a room temperature mushroom cap on top of each slice

Garnish with extra chopped thyme if desired and serve.

Long Island Iced Tea
(Per drink)

1 oz vodka
1 oz Tequila
1 oz rum
1 oz gin
1 oz triple sec
1 splash of regular cola (not diet)

1. Put all the ingredients in a shaker with ice and give one brisk shake
2. Pour into a tall glass
3. Garnish with lemon slice (optional)

 # Wine

Tim recommends serving a medium-bodied red wine with this menu such as a fruity Côtes du Rhône from the southern Rhône Valley in France or a Spanish Ribeiro del Duero.

Nan Kicks Jim Out of the Kitchen

Recently, Nan decided to host a jewelry party for good friend Lynne Van Ness. Now, I had no idea what a jewelry party was, I only heard "twenty women at Sunny Shores" and "buffet supper." I assumed Nan would want me to do the cooking and I already had cooking classes and a dinner party planned for that same week. I started to complain, just a bit, when Nan cut me off and said she planned to do all the cooking and Marjorie was going to bring dessert. Nan strongly suggested I stay out of her way and make myself scarce for the entire evening. What? I'm the chef in this house!

On the evening of the jewelry party, as I was leaving, Nan was busy in our little kitchen making chicken Caesar salads and a beautiful tomato salad for twenty.

Well, for days afterwards I heard from several women how much they enjoyed the party and how fabulous the food had been. Many assumed I had done the cooking but I was happy to tell them, "No, Nan was the chef that night." I just wish Marjorie hadn't told me Nan's Caesar salad dressing was an improvement over mine -- I think she added more anchovies. Nan really is a good cook. I just wish she would do it a little more often. Oh, and Marjorie knows where to buy the best sorbet in the county (Hill Top Soda Shoppe in Benzonia).

Menu X

Nan's Party
(Serves 8)

Nan's Spinach Rounds

Golden Cheddar Bon Bons

Turkey Pâté in Endive

Zucchini Puffs

Kiwi & Strawberry Kabobs

Champagne Celebration Cocktails

The recipe for the spinach rounds is a specialty of Nan's which she has prepared many times. The other recipes, except the Kiwi & Strawberry Kabobs, in this chapter are from various friends of Nan's that she has known for many years. I created the kiwi recipe especially for Nan because of her love for kiwis and strawberries. The special drink is another of Nan's favorites.

Nan's Spinach Rounds

2 packages chopped frozen spinach

2 cups packaged herb bread stuffing

2 medium yellow onions

6 large eggs

$\frac{3}{4}$ cup freshly grated Parmesan cheese (about 6 oz)

2 garlic cloves

Golden Cheddar Bon Bons

12 oz freshly grated Cheddar cheese

1 8-oz package cream cheese

$\frac{1}{4}$ tsp chili powder

$\frac{1}{2}$ tsp dry mustard

2 Tbls dry sherry

1 bunch fresh parsley

Turkey Pâté in Endive

1 pound smoked turkey (you can use packaged turkey from the deli)

8 oz chopped walnuts

$\frac{1}{2}$ cup sour cream

$\frac{1}{2}$ cup mayonnaise

$\frac{1}{4}$ cup ($\frac{1}{2}$ stick) unsalted butter

1 small yellow onion

4 heads Belgian endive

Zucchini Puffs

2 medium zucchinis

$\frac{1}{3}$ cup freshly grated parmesan cheese

$\frac{1}{3}$ cup mayonnaise

1 small bunch fresh basil

Kiwi & Strawberry Kabobs

12 medium strawberries

6 large kiwis

8 fresh basil leaves

$\frac{1}{2}$ cup sugar

24 decorative toothpicks

Champagne Celebration Cocktail

Cointreau

Brandy

Sugar cubes

Bitters

Champagne

Nan's Spinach Rounds
(Makes 36 pieces)

1. Thaw and drain thoroughly, 2 packages of chopped frozen spinach

2. Preheat oven to 350 degrees Fahrenheit

3. In a large bowl, beat 6 large eggs well

4. Add the following ingredients and mix well:
   a. 2 cups packaged herb bread stuffing
   b. 2 medium yellow onions, minced
   c. $\frac{3}{4}$ cup freshly grated Parmesan cheese (about 6 oz)
   d. 2 garlic cloves, minced
   e. The 2 packages of thawed and drained chopped spinach

5. Dampen your hands lightly and form mixture into small balls

6. Place on nonstick baking pan and bake for 20 minutes or until lightly browned

Serve warm or at room temperature.

Golden Cheddar Bon Bons
(Makes 36 pieces)

1. Blend the following ingredients in medium bowl until smooth:
   a. 12 oz freshly grated Cheddar cheese
   b. 8 oz of room temperature cream cheese
   c. $\frac{1}{4}$ tsp chili powder
   d. $\frac{1}{2}$ tsp dry mustard
   e. 2 Tbls dry sherry

2. Cover bowl and chill for several hours or overnight

3. Roll mixture into small balls about 1 inch in diameter

4. Finely chop 1 bunch fresh parsley

5. Roll balls in chopped parsley and chill until serving

Serve at room temperature.

Turkey Pâté in Endive

(Makes 24 pieces)

1. Put 8-oz walnuts in food processor and pulse until finely chopped

2. Add the following ingredients and process until smooth:

   a. 1 pound smoked turkey, chopped

   b. $\frac{1}{2}$ cup sour cream

   c. $\frac{1}{2}$ cup mayonnaise

   d. $\frac{1}{4}$ cup ($\frac{1}{2}$ stick) room temperature unsalted butter

   e. 1 Tbls minced yellow onion

3. Transfer to a bowl, cover and chill for several hours or overnight. Return to room temperature before piping.

4. Separate endive leaves from 4 heads of Belgian endive (you should get 6 good leaves per head)

5. Put pâté mixture in a piping bag with a medium tip, or in a plastic bag and cut the tip off one corner. Pipe one heaping teaspoon of mix on each leaf.

Return to refrigerator and chill until serving.

Zucchini Puffs
(Makes 24 pieces)

1. Clean, dry and slice 2 medium zucchinis into 12 pieces each

2. Combine the following ingredients in a small bowl and mix well:

    a. $\frac{1}{3}$ cup freshly grated Parmesan cheese

    b. $\frac{1}{3}$ cup mayonnaise

    c. 1 tsp finely chopped fresh basil

3. Cover and chill mixture for several hours or overnight

4. Spread a thin layer of mixture on each zucchini slice

5. Preheat broiler

6. Place zucchini slices on broiler pan and broil about 5 inches below heat for 30 to 40 seconds

7. Watch carefully, they turn golden very quickly

Serve warm or at room temperature.

NOTES

Kiwi & Strawberry Kabobs

(Makes 24 pieces)

1. Make simple sugar syrup by bringing $\frac{1}{2}$ cup sugar and $\frac{1}{2}$ cup water to a boil

2. Take off heat and let cool to room temperature

3. Clean and cut 12 medium strawberries in half

4. Peel and cut 6 large kiwis into quarters

5. Chiffonade 8 fresh basil leaves

6. Put $\frac{1}{4}$ kiwi on toothpick add $\frac{1}{2}$ strawberry followed by a $\frac{1}{4}$ kiwi

7. Place all kabobs on serving platter and drizzle with sugar syrup

Sprinkle basil over kabobs and chill until serving.

Champagne Celebration

(Per drink)

½ oz Cointreau
½ oz brandy
1 sugar cube saturated with a splash of bitters
4 oz champagne

1. Place sugar cube, Cointreau and brandy in champagne flute
2. Pour champagne over and serve

 # Wine

Tim says this menu calls for a rosé wine such as Roditis or a similar medium rosé. If you prefer a white wine, the deep golden color, complex aroma, and fruity taste of a Viognier; or a drier white Spanish Albariño wine would also pair well.

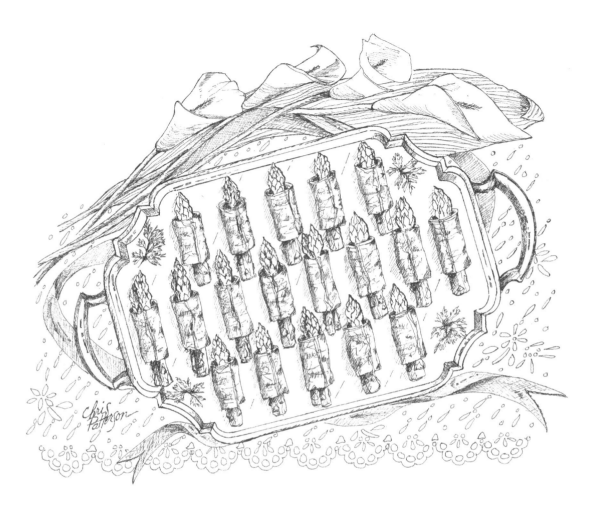

Jennifer Makes a Wedding Commitment

Jennifer Mills is my good friend Betsie Hosick's niece and a regular visitor to Crystal Lake. After returning to her home in Massachusetts last summer, Jennifer was invited to a wedding and interestingly enough, the wedding reception was Pot Luck. Jennifer committed to making one of my recipes, asparagus wrapped in filo, as an hors d'œuvre for the dinner. She thought this was a great idea until she found out there were going to be 125 people at the reception. Jennifer had never worked with filo dough before and soon found out that if you don't thaw the dough enough it will crack, leaving a mess and not much to show for your efforts; and if you let it dry out too much, the same phenomenon occurs. By the end of her first day of rolling asparagus, Jennifer had decided that my recommendation of always preparing three pieces per person was not necessary; one per person would do just fine. Two days, six pounds of asparagus, one pound of butter, a large piece of Parmesan cheese and two boxes of filo dough later, she had her dish to bring.

The next party menu includes the recipe for asparagus wrapped in filo dough. I guarantee your guests will love it; just plan on serving it at smaller parties unless you have a lot of time and patience.

Menu XI

Make a Commitment
(Serves 8)

Asparagus in Filo (Phyllo)

Three Mushroom Pâté

Goat Cheese Caviar Ball

Tomato & Feta Toast

Crab Deviled Eggs

Tom Collins Cocktails

Jennifer acted as sous chef for three of my classes last July and has a great commitment to good cooking. This is probably the most elegant and most time consuming menu in the whole book and is perfectly suited to a wedding reception or any other occasion which fits an upscale presentation. Everything but the tomato/feta toast can be prepared in advance and kept chilled until serving.

Asparagus in Filo

1 package filo (phyllo) dough

36 small to medium asparagus spears

8 oz Parmesan cheese

1 stick unsalted butter

Three Mushroom Pâté

6 oz each of shitake, morel, and chanterelle mushrooms
(You can substitute with cremini, wood ear or portobellos (not baby))

2 Tbls unsalted butter

1 medium sweet onion

1 tsp minced garlic

½ cup dry white wine

1 small bunch fresh thyme

1 bunch fresh parsley

1 tsp truffle oil (you can substitute a very good first pressed olive oil)

3 oz cream cheese

3 oz plain goat cheese

1 French baguette or bread of your choice for toasting

Salt and pepper

Goat Cheese Caviar Ball

2 8-oz packages cream cheese

1 6-oz package unflavored goat cheese

1 small white onion

2 large eggs

1 Tbls mayonnaise

2 jars black whitefish caviar (or caviar of your choice)

1 French baguette or bread of your choice for toasting

Tomato & Feta Toast

1 French baguette

1 bunch fresh basil

1 jar sundried tomatoes in oil

8 oz natural unflavored feta cheese

Anchovies or capers (your choice, you could use rolled anchovies with capers)

Pepper

Crab Deviled Eggs

12 large eggs

4 Tbls mascarpone cheese

2 Tbls sour cream

2 Tbls mayonnaise

2 Tbls Dijon mustard

2 lemons

1 tsp celery salt

1 bunch fresh chives

12 oz lump crab meat

Salt and pepper

Tom Collins Cocktails

Vodka

Lemons

Powdered sugar

Soda water

Maraschino cherries and orange slices for garnish

Asparagus in Filo (Phyllo)
(Makes 36 pieces)

1. Preheat oven to 375 degrees Fahrenheit

2. Take 1 sheet of thawed filo dough from package, open onto a damp towel and cut in half

3. Keep dough covered with a damp towel during preparation

4. Take one $\frac{1}{2}$ sheet at a time and place on cutting board

5. Brush lightly with melted butter

6. Place 1 asparagus spear on the dough leaving approximately 1 inch of the flower outside of dough and enough dough on the other end to fold over asparagus

7. Sprinkle with 1 tsp of the freshly grated parmesan cheese

8. Fold the exposed dough over the bottom of the asparagus and roll into a cylinder

9. Place on a nonstick baking pan, seam side down

10. Repeat until all spears are rolled in filo

11. Brush lightly with melted butter and sprinkle remaining cheese over top of dough

12. Bake for approximately 15 to 20 minutes, until lightly browned

Serve warm or at room temperature.

This recipe can be completely done up to the baking point, hours or even 1 day ahead. Just cover the rolled asparagus with a damp towel and cover with plastic wrap. Refrigerate until ready to bake but remove from refrigerator and bring to room temperature before baking.

Three Mushroom Pâté

(Serves 8)

This recipe should be prepared one day in advance.

1. Clean, trim the stems, and roughly chop:
    a. 6 oz shitake mushrooms
    b. 6 oz morel mushrooms
    c. 6 oz chanterelle mushrooms
        (You can substitute with cremini, wood ear
        or portobellos (not baby))

2. Melt 2 Tbls unsalted butter in a large skillet over medium high heat

3. Add 2 Tbls finely chopped sweet onions and 1 tsp minced garlic

4. Sauté until onions are tender (about 3 minutes)

5. Add the chopped mushrooms and sauté until lightly browned
    (about 5 minutes)

6. Add:
    a. $\frac{1}{2}$ cup dry white wine
    b. 1 tsp minced fresh thyme
    c. $\frac{1}{2}$ tsp salt and $\frac{1}{4}$ tsp pepper

7. Stir and cook until wine is nearly evaporated (about 5 minutes)

8. Add 2 Tbls chopped fresh parsley and 1 tsp truffle oil

9. Cook for 30 seconds

10. Transfer to a food processor, add 3 oz of room temperature
    cream cheese and 3 oz of room temperature goat cheese

11. Blend until well combined

12. Check seasoning for taste

13. Transfer to a decorative bowl or cassolette, cover and chill for at
    least 4 hours

Serve chilled or at room temperature with toast points or toasted
baguette slices.

Goat Cheese Caviar Ball

(Serves 8)

This recipe is courtesy of Jeri Richardson from her mother.

1. Put the following in a bowl and mix together:

    a.   2 8-oz packages of room temperature cream cheese

    b.   1 6-oz package of room temperature goat cheese

    c.   ½ cup minced white onion

    d.   Minced egg whites from 2 large hardboiled eggs

    e.   1 Tbls mayonnaise

2. Form into a ball, place back into bowl, cover and refrigerate until firm or overnight

You can complete recipe to this point and keep refrigerated for up to 2 days.

3. When ready to serve, place cheese ball on decorative platter

4. Thoroughly drain 2 jars of black whitefish caviar (or caviar of choice)

5. Carefully cover the ball completely with caviar

Serve with toast points or toasted baguette slices.

Tomato & Feta Toast

(Makes about 24 pieces)

This should not be prepared more than a few hours before serving as toast may become soggy.

1. Slice 1 French baguette into ½ inch thick pieces and lightly toast

2. Put 1 basil leaf on each baguette slice

3. Drain one jar of sundried tomatoes in oil and place a piece of sundried tomato on top of the basil leaf

4. Top tomato with a small slice unflavored feta cheese

5. Put either a caper or small piece of anchovy on top

6. Sprinkle with fresh cracked black pepper

Serve at room temperature on decorative plate.

Crab Deviled Eggs

(Makes 24 pieces)

1. Hard boil 12 large eggs, cool, peel, and cut in half lengthwise. (For the best hardboiled eggs, put 12 room temperature eggs in a pan large enough so eggs are not stacked and not touching, cover with cool water, bring to a light boil, remove from heat, cover and let stand for 12 minutes, drain and fill pan with cold water 2 or 3 times to cool eggs, immediately crack and peel. You can store peeled eggs in a plastic bag in the refrigerator for 24 hours.)

2. Remove the yolks and save for another use, set whites aside

3. Put the following into a large bowl and mix together:

   a. 4 Tbls mascarpone cheese

   b. 2 Tbls sour cream

   c. 2 Tbls mayonnaise

   d. 2 Tbls Dijon mustard

   e. 2 Tbls fresh lemon juice

   f. 1 tsp salt and $\frac{1}{2}$ tsp pepper

   g. 1 tsp celery salt

   h. 2 Tbls finely diced fresh chives

4. Check 12 oz lump crab meat for shells, chop and add to mixture

5. Using a teaspoon, put crab mixture into egg halves

Chill until serving.

Tom Collins

(Per drink)

2 oz vodka
Juice of 1 small lemon
1 tsp powdered sugar
Soda water
1 maraschino cherry and 1 orange slice for garnish

1. Put vodka, lemon juice, powdered sugar, and ice in a shaker

2. Shake well and strain into a tall glass with ice

3. Fill with soda water and top with a cherry and orange slice

 # Wine

Tim says the food pairing versatility and refreshing palate of a dry Riesling or Pinot Gris makes either one of these two white wines a good choice to complement this menu.

Jim Entertains Thirteen Women

Last summer, a new friend, Peggy Burns, planned a weekend party for twelve of her friends as part of a high school class reunion and celebration of a certain birthday (hint: class of 1978). She wanted me to be part of the entertainment. . . I did a private cooking class for the group on Peggy's delightful and eclectic side porch. The menu I designed had to meet Peggy's three requirements: be unforgettable, incorporate local ingredients, and easy to replicate. We decided on six hors d'œuvres (recipes for all can be found in this book); Baked Shrimp, Asparagus in Prosciutto, Endive with Stilton, Goat Cheese Stuffed Fingerling Potatoes, Betsie Bay Smoked Lake Trout Pâté, and Stuffed Cherry Tomatoes. Lemoncillo martinis to start the evening and a Yogurt Cake and Chocolate Torte dessert course completed the menu.

The porch looked great. Peggy set up a long table, converted from the old Frankfort Golf Course sign, and covered it with an old fashioned print tablecloth. She spread the porch with a few feather boas, lots of candles and a sparkling array of white lights. Serving ware featured a "cottage mix" of dishes and glasses, and lots of wine bottles. I had four different wines to pair with the hors d'œuvres, but wanting a bit more sparkle to end the evening, Peggy requested dessert be served with a local wine called Sex. Yes, the name of the wine really is Sex. It's a nice Mawby sparkling wine from the Leelanau Peninsula . . . but imagine how I felt with thirteen women constantly asking me for more Sex! . . . I had a great time.

If Peggy has another party next summer, I might recommend the following menu; it would pair well with the Sex.

Menu XII

A Very Entertaining Menu
(Serves 8)

Celery with Caviar

Parmesan Crisps

Mini Quiches

Marinated Pork Strips

Marinated Raw Mushrooms

Singapore Sling Cocktails

The marinated pork strips are my version of a mini Asian spare rib without the bone and with a lot less mess. I really like the addition of the salty caviar and crisp Parmesan strips from my first book "Dinner on the Porch". Everything but the Parmesan crisps can be prepared the day before and kept cool until serving. The crisps can be prepared early on the party day and left on the counter if it is not too humid, otherwise store in a plastic bag.

Celery with Caviar

1 bunch celery hearts

1 8-oz package cream cheese

1 small jar red caviar

1 small sweet onion

1 bunch fresh parsley

Salt and pepper

Parmesan Crisps

16 oz Parmesan cheese

Mini Quiches

24 bite size puff pastry cups (There are usually 12 per bag)

4 large eggs

$1\frac{1}{2}$ cups heavy cream

$\frac{1}{2}$ cup freshly grated Parmesan cheese

$\frac{1}{4}$ tsp white pepper

$\frac{1}{8}$ tsp freshly grated nutmeg

Salt

Marinated Pork Strips

1 pork tenderloin, about 1 pound

$\frac{1}{2}$ cup soy sauce

2 garlic cloves

3 Tbls sugar

1 small yellow onion

2 Tbls freshly ground ginger

$\frac{1}{2}$ cup sesame seeds

2 Tbls olive oil (extra virgin not necessary)

Decorative toothpicks

Marinated Raw Mushrooms

24 very small baby portobello mushrooms

$\frac{1}{2}$ cup extra virgin olive oil

1 lemon

$\frac{1}{2}$ tsp dried oregano

Salt and pepper

Decorative toothpicks

Singapore Sling Cocktails

Gin

Cherry brandy

Grenadine

Soda water

Sour mix

Maraschino cherries

Celery with Caviar
(Makes 24 pieces)

Use only the best inner stalks of celery, usually 4 stalks will be enough for 24 2-inch pieces

1. Wash and dry 4 stalks of celery and cut a very thin slice off the back so they will not roll over when filled

2. Cut the stalks into 24 2-inch pieces and place on a dry surface

3. Combine the following in a medium bowl and mix well:

    a. 1 8-oz package room temperature cream cheese

    b. 1 small jar red caviar

    c. 1 Tbls minced sweet onion

    d. $\frac{1}{3}$ cup chopped fresh parsley

    e. $\frac{1}{2}$ tsp salt

    f. $\frac{1}{4}$ tsp freshly ground black pepper

4. Pipe the mixture into the celery pieces and chill until serving

Parmesan Crisps
(Makes 24 pieces)

You must use a nonstick baking pan lined with parchment paper or Silpat for this recipe.

1. Preheat oven to 350 degrees Fahrenheit

2. Grate 16 oz fresh Parmesan cheese with semi-fine grater

3. Place heaping tablespoons of the grated cheese separated on nonstick baking pan lined with parchment paper or Silpat.

4. Bake for 15 to 20 minutes until golden brown

5. Remove from oven and cool on a wire rack

These are best served within a few hours.

NOTES

Mini Quiches

(Makes 24 pieces)

1. Preheat oven to 375 degrees Fahrenheit

2. Place 24 bite size puff pastry cups on a nonstick baking sheet

3. In a large bowl, beat 4 large eggs well

4. Add:

    a. $1\frac{1}{2}$ cups heavy cream

    b. $\frac{1}{2}$ cup freshly grated parmesan cheese

    c. $\frac{1}{2}$ tsp salt

    d. $\frac{1}{4}$ tsp white pepper

    e. $\frac{1}{8}$ tsp freshly grated nutmeg

5. Pour mixture into a large container with a pouring spout and fill pastry cups

6. Bake for about 20 minutes until firm

Chill, and then bring to room temperature before serving.

Marinated Pork Strips

(Makes about 32 pieces)

1. Trim any fat from 1 pound pork tenderloin, split lengthwise and put in large plastic bag

2. In a separate bowl, combine:

    a. $\frac{1}{2}$ cup soy sauce
    b. 2 garlic cloves, minced
    c. 3 Tbls sugar
    d. 2 Tbls minced yellow onion
    e. 2 Tbls freshly ground ginger
    f. $\frac{1}{2}$ cup sesame seeds
    g. 2 Tbls olive oil

3. Pour mixture over pork

4. Seal bag and marinate in the refrigerator for 3 to 4 hours

5. Preheat oven to 375 degrees Fahrenheit

6. Drain pork, reserving the marinade, and place in a roasting pan

7. Bake until tender, about 15 to 20 minutes, but do not over cook

8. Meanwhile simmer the reserved marinade on medium heat until reduced by one half

9. Take meat from oven, baste with cooked marinade and cool to room temperature

10. Chill pork until serving

Cut into very thin slices and serve with decorative toothpicks.

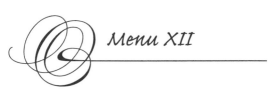

Marinated Raw Mushrooms
(Makes 24 pieces)

NOTES

1. Cut the stems from 24 very small baby portobello mushrooms and wipe clean with a cloth or paper towel

2. Put mushrooms in a large plastic bag

3. In a separate bowl, combine:

   a. $\frac{1}{2}$ cup extra virgin olive oil

   b. 3 Tbls fresh lemon juice

   c. $\frac{1}{2}$ tsp dried oregano

   d. $\frac{1}{2}$ tsp salt

   e. $\frac{1}{4}$ tsp freshly ground black pepper

4. Pour marinade over mushrooms

5. Seal bag and marinate at room temperature for at least 6 to 8 hours

Chill, then drain and bring to room temperature before serving. This recipe can be made up to a day in advance and refrigerated. Serve with decorative toothpicks.

Singapore Sling
(Per drink)

1 oz gin
1½ oz cherry brandy
½ oz grenadine
2½ oz soda water
1 oz sour mix
1 maraschino cherry

1. Put gin, brandy, grenadine, soda water, sour mix and ice in shaker

2. Shake well and strain into tall glass with ice

3. Garnish with maraschino cherry

 **Wine**

A sparkling wine is Tim's first choice for this festive menu; Champagne, Cava, or Prosecco would all work beautifully as would a light and fresh and slightly effervescent Vinho Verde. Of course, there's also the sparkling Mawby called "Sex" from Michigan to consider.

Cooking Classes in an Old Drugstore

Jeanne Sitter, a frequent student in my cooking classes, asked me if I would do a private class for "The Ladies of Arcadia." I was quite flattered since I knew Jeanne had managed the cooking school at Rice Epicurean Markets in Houston and had been a sous chef for some of the best chefs in the city before retiring. I soon found out that the "Ladies of Arcadia" was a wonderful group of women who live in or near the small town of Arcadia, about 15 miles south of Frankfort. Outside of their families, careers, and volunteer work, these women like to have a good time (Jeanne suggested I bring a couple extra bottles of wine for the Arcadia classes).

One of Jeanne's good friends, Charlene Lang, bought the old Arcadia drugstore and made it into her home a few years ago. From the outside, it still looks very much like the old store; so much so, Charlene had to hang a sign on the door saying "This is now a private residence." But inside, she's transformed it into a lovely home. The old soda fountain is now a wonderful kitchen, perfect for our cooking classes. Charlene, a retired music teacher, added a unique feature to her living room, an old pipe organ, which she will play if coaxed during class breaks. After my first Arcadia class, Jeanne presented me with a sign that says "Welcome To The Porch" and it now hangs above the screen door on the porch at Sunny Shores. What a great time.

Menu XIII

Ye Olde Drugstore Party
(Serves 8)

Crisp Pecans

Buttered Radishes

Artichoke Bottoms with Crabmeat

Melon & Kiwi Wrapped in Prosciutto

Asian Tea Eggs

Tequila Sunrise Cocktails

This menu adds a touch of the flavors from the Orient and has a really great variety of textures. Radishes are a very underutilized vegetable and are great not only to eat, but for decorating. They have a spicy flavor much different from a green onion and can be made into rosettes as done in this menu. The Asian tea egg will give a whole new concept to hard-boiled eggs.

Crisp Pecans

1 pound unsalted pecan halves

½ cup sugar

Olive oil (extra virgin
not necessary)

Salt

Buttered Radishes

24 medium sized radishes

1 3-oz package cream cheese

1 stick unsalted butter

1 bunch fresh chives

Salt

Artichoke Bottoms with Crabmeat

4 cans artichoke bottoms
(there are usually 6 per can)

1 pound lump crabmeat

1 heaping Tbls mayonnaise

1 lemon

4 shallots

1 small jar pimentos

Salt

Melon & Kiwi Wrapped in Prosciutto

1 large cantaloupe

12 small Kiwis

24 thin slices Prosciutto

24 decorative toothpicks

Asian Tea Eggs

12 large eggs

¼ cup Sake

3 Tbls soy sauce

½ cup black tea leaves

2 Tbls crushed fresh ginger

2 cinnamon sticks

2 oranges

3 star anise

Salt

Tequila Sunrise Cocktails

Tequila

Fresh squeezed orange juice

Grenadine

Crisp Pecans
(Serves 8)

1. Bring 4 cups of water, ½ cup sugar and 1 tsp salt to a boil

2. Add 1 pound unsalted pecan halves and return to a boil

3. Reduce heat and cook uncovered for 15 minutes

4. Drain pecans well and spread in a single layer on baking pan

5. Let dry for at least 1 hour

6. Preheat oven to 300 degrees Fahrenheit

7. Lightly grease a baking pan with olive oil

8. Spread dried nuts on greased pan in single layer and bake for 45 minutes until crisp

Cool completely and serve at room temperature. You can store nuts tightly covered for up to 5 days before serving.

Buttered Radishes

(Makes 24 pieces)

1. Wash 24 medium sized radishes, cut off the stem and cut a small slice from the bottom so they sit flat

2. Cut radishes into rosettes. You make rosettes by making a thin slice 2/3 of the way down 4 sides of the radish.

3. Put radishes in a bowl with ice water and 1 Tbls salt; radishes will "blossom" into rosettes in the salt water

4. Put in the refrigerator and chill overnight

5. Combine 1 3-oz package of room temperature cream cheese and 1 stick of unsalted room temperature butter and mix well

6. Take the radishes from the ice water but do not rinse. Set on paper towels to drain.

7. Cut off a small piece of the white center part of the radish

8. Pipe the butter mixture into the center of the radish

9. Top with a sprinkle of minced chives

Keep chilled until serving.

Artichoke Bottoms with Crabmeat
(Makes 24 pieces)

1. Drain 4 cans artichoke bottoms (should be 24 pieces) and dry artichoke bottoms on paper towels

2. Put 1 pound of lump crabmeat in bowl, checking for any shells and break into small pieces

3. Add the following and mix:
   a. 1 heaping Tbls mayonnaise
   b. The juice of one lemon
   c. 4 shallots, minced (about 2 Tbls)
   d. 1 tsp salt

4. Equally mound the crabmeat mixture on the artichoke bottoms

5. Put a small piece of pimento on top, cover and chill until serving

Melon & Kiwi Wrapped in Prosciutto
(Makes 24 pieces)

1. Cut one large cantaloupe in half, discard the seeds and cut 24 one inch rounds using a melon baller

2. Peel 12 small kiwis and cut in half

3. Wrap the melon piece and kiwi in one thin slice of prosciutto and pierce with a decorative toothpick

4. Cover and chill until serving

Asian Tea Eggs

(Makes 48 pieces)

1. Bring 12 large eggs to room temperature

2. Put the room temperature eggs in a pot covered with cool water

3. Bring to a boil, reduce heat to low and simmer for 10 minutes uncovered

4. Drain and let cool in cold water, drain again and lightly tap eggs on hard surface to crack shells, but do not peel

5. Put the following ingredients in a large pot:

    a. $\frac{1}{4}$ cup Sake

    b. 3 Tbls soy sauce

    c. $\frac{1}{2}$ cup black tea leaves

    d. 2 Tbls crushed fresh ginger

    e. 2 cinnamon sticks

    f. The peel of 2 oranges

    g. 3 star anise

    h. $1\frac{1}{2}$ Tbls salt

6. Bring to boil over high heat, reduce heat to low and simmer for 20 minutes

7. Add the cracked eggs and continue to simmer for another 45 minutes

8. Remove from heat and let cool to room temperature in tea mixture

9. Remove eggs and peel

Chill, but bring to room temperature and quarter eggs into wedges before serving.

Tequila Sunrise
(Per drink)

2 oz tequila
6 oz fresh squeezed orange juice
2 dashes grenadine

1. Put tequila in a tall glass filled with ice

2. Top with the orange juice and stir

3. Put the 2 dashes of Grenadine on top

4. Garnish with a slice of orange (optional)

 # Wine

Tim says this menu calls for a fruity
and spicy white wine such as a highly aromatic
and spicy Gewurztraminer; a German Riesling;
or a fruity, floral, and utterly charming
Torrontes from Argentina.

Jim Prepares Salmon Again... and Again... and Again

Lynne Van Ness and Woodgie Logan have been best friends and friends of mine since childhood. I even dated both Lynne and Woodgie briefly during and after college, when they were Lynne Herrmann and Woodgie Smolik. I find myself still identifying them as Herrmann and Smolik. (With five ex-husbands between the two of them it's hard to keep up and safer to just stick with their maiden names.)

Last summer Lynne's two sons and grandson were visiting and I invited her whole family, Woodgie, and several others we've known all our lives over for grilled fish. Lynne insisted on providing the fish. Her sons and grandson had been fishing on Lake Michigan and they wanted me to have all the fish they caught. Lynne assured me they had enough for a large dinner party. I needn't have worried. Everyone had caught the limit and they had an abundance of beautiful fresh King Salmon, far more than even the fourteen guests at our dinner party could eat. I had enough for a second dinner party the next night with new friends and neighbors, Carol and Jeff Barbour. (The Barbours are from Connecticut where they own an upscale wine shop. They brought several bottles of exclusive wines for us to sample along with dinner. Fabulous!) Even after two dinner parties, we had fish in the freezer for weeks. Nan and I had grilled fish, poached fish, and even made gravlax (from my first cookbook "Dinner on the Porch"). I'll echo what Bob Weber says, "We live well, don't we."

Menu XIV

Lynn's Party
(Serves 8)

Fennel Wrapped in Prosciutto

New Potatoes with Sour Cream and Bacon

Chicken Bites

Cherry Tomatoes with Stilton

Cherries & Grapes

Mai Tai Cocktails

This is another really great example of a complete dinner party menu turned into an hors d'œuvres party. It has all the courses; from the fennel appetizer to the cherry and grape dessert, with a main course of chicken and two vegetables in between. Everything in this menu can be prepared in advance, even the day before the party, just bring the potatoes and chicken bites to room temperature before serving.

Shopping List

Fennel Wrapped in Prosciutto

1 large fennel bulb

24 thin slices of prosciutto

4 oz Parmesan cheese

Extra virgin olive oil

Pepper

Decorative toothpicks

New Potatoes with Sour Cream and Bacon

12 small new potatoes (red skinned)

6 oz sour cream

2 oz cream cheese

6 strips pepper bacon

Salt

Chicken Bites

1 pound chicken tenders (6 tenders)

½ cup milk

1 large egg

Vegetable oil for deep frying

½ cup dry seasoned bread crumbs

½ cup cornmeal

½ cup flour

6 Tbls honey

¼ cup Dijon mustard

Salt and Pepper

Decorative toothpicks

Cherry Tomatoes with Stilton

24 cherry tomatoes

6 oz Stilton Bleu cheese

2 oz unsalted butter (4 Tbls)

Cherries & Grapes

1 pound fresh cherries, mixed varieties

1 pound grapes, mixed varieties

Decorative lettuce

Mai Tai Cocktails

Dark rum

Light rum

Triple sec

Fresh orange juice

Fresh lemon juice

Pineapple juice

Limes

Fennel Wrapped in Prosciutto
(Makes 24 pieces)

1. Trim the top and bottom from one large fennel bulb

2. Cut the bulb in half vertically, then cut halves crosswise into thin pieces

3. You should get at least 24 slices

4. Wrap each fennel slice in a thin slice of prosciutto and secure with a decorative toothpick

5. Place pieces on a platter, sprinkle with olive oil

6. Sprinkle with 4 oz of freshly grated Parmesan cheese

7. Sprinkle with freshly ground black pepper

Chill, but bring to room temperature before serving.

New Potatoes with Sour Cream and Bacon

(Makes 24 pieces)

1. Wash and cut 12 small new potatoes in half crosswise

2. Using a melon baller or small spoon scoop out the center of the potato leaving plenty of potato with skin

3. Place potatoes in pot covered with water and 1 Tbls salt

4. Bring to a boil, reduce heat to low boil and cook for 6 to 8 minutes until tender but still firm, do not overcook, put in an ice bath to cool, then drain

5. Fry 6 strips of pepper bacon until crisp and drain

6. Mix $\frac{3}{4}$ cup (6 oz) sour cream with 2 oz room temperature cream cheese until smooth

7. Using a piping bag or a plastic bag with one corner cut off, pipe cheese mixture into chilled potatoes

8. Top with crumbled bacon lightly pressed into cheese

Keep chilled until serving.

Chicken Bites
(Makes 24 pieces)

1. Cut 6 chicken tenders into 1 inch bite size pieces, about 4 pieces per tender

2. In a large bowl, whisk together:
   a. $\frac{1}{2}$ cup milk
   b. 1 large egg
   c. 1 Tbls vegetable oil
   d. 1 Tbls water

3. Put chicken pieces in milk mixture and coat completely

4. In another large bowl, combine:
   a. $\frac{1}{2}$ cup dry seasoned bread crumbs
   b. $\frac{1}{2}$ cup cornmeal
   c. $\frac{1}{2}$ cup flour
   d. 1 tsp salt
   e. $\frac{1}{2}$ tsp freshly ground pepper

5. Take chicken pieces a few at a time and put into dry mixture, coating all sides

6. Put coated chicken pieces on a wire rack to dry for 15 minutes

7. Heat vegetable oil in deep fryer or 2 inches deep in frying pan to 375 degrees Fahrenheit

8. Fry chicken bites until golden brown, about 3 to 4 minutes, do not crowd pan

9. Drain on paper towels and serve warm or at room temperature with your choice of sauce, I suggest a honey/mustard sauce:
   a. Mix 6 Tbls honey with $\frac{1}{4}$ cup Dijon mustard
   b. Drizzle over chicken bites

Serve with decorative toothpicks and a bowl for discarded toothpicks.

Cherry Tomatoes with Stilton
(Makes 24 pieces)

1. Wash and dry 24 cherry tomatoes

2. Cut the top $\frac{1}{3}$ off the tomatoes and discard

3. Using a small spoon or melon baller scoop out the tomato pulp

4. Turn the tomatoes upside down on paper towels to drain

5. Combine 6 oz room temperature Stilton Bleu cheese with 2 oz (4 Tbls) room temperature unsalted butter and mix until smooth. This can be done in a small food processor.

6. Using a piping bag or a plastic bag with a corner snipped off, pipe the cheese mixture into the tomatoes and chill until serving

Cherries & Grapes
(Serves 8)

1. Wash and dry 1 pound of fresh cherries and 1 pound of fresh grapes

2. Cut the grapes into small bunches of 3 to 4 grapes each

3. Place cherries and grapes on platter decorated with lettuce

4. Chill until serving

Mai Tai
(Per drink)

1½ oz dark rum
1½ oz light rum
¾ oz triple sec
½ oz fresh orange juice
½ oz fresh lemon juice
2 oz pineapple juice
1 lime wedge

1. Squeeze lime wedge and leave in tall glass filled with ice

2. Put all other ingredients in a shaker and shake well

3. Pour into the tall glass filled with ice

 # Wine

Tim recommends a crisp, elegant and fresh Sauvignon Blanc or a non-oaky Chardonnay with this menu. If you prefer a red wine, he recommends choosing a fruity light red wine such as Brouilly.

NOTES

Five Rabbits, Twenty Guests, and Fancy Placards

Last year I wanted to do a really special "end of summer" dinner, and decided to do five different international gourmet prepared rabbits with help from four of my good friends. Our menu consisted of: Conejo en Salas de Chocolate (Spanish) by Kim Fairchild, Coniglio Sorpreso (Italian) by Jeri Richardson, Hassenpfeffer (German) by Larry "Lars" Hilton and Beth Tabbert, Rabbit Braised in Oregano Pinot Gris (American) by Leslie McGrath, and Le Lapin au Moutarde (French) by me.

Side dishes served included: ratatouille, spaetzel, delicata squash, Mediterranean vegetables en casserole, a fresh tomato garden salad and a special spicy carrot dish. All of this was followed by an unbelievable coffee ice cream Baked Alaska also by Lars and Beth. (Marjorie insisted that she wanted to contribute to the menu as well. Thinking quickly, I suggested she make fancy placards to place on the table to identify the dishes.)

To accommodate the twenty sit-down dinner guests in this little cottage, we set up a table for ten in the living room and sat ten on the porch. We had a wonderful time, the food was fabulous, the cottage cozy, and the placards looked great. It became a general conclusion that we could have served the Delicata squash and the spiced carrots as hors d'œuvres and still had plenty of side dishes. You'll find the recipes for them in the next menu.

Menu XV

Rabbit Night
(Serves 6)

Baked Delicata Squash Rings

Spiced Carrots

Mini Crab Cakes

Portobello Mushrooms Stuffed with Sausage

Puff Pastry Parmesan Strips

Cosmopolitan Martinis

This is a great example of a complete dinner menu transformed into hors d'œuvres. It would even work for vegetarians who eat seafood. If they don't eat meat, just substitute the Endive with Stilton and Walnuts from Menu IV for the Stuffed Portobello Mushrooms. The many flavors and textures in this menu make a great visual presentation for your guests. They will be anticipating the great tastes before they take the first bite.

I've paired this menu with Cosmopolitan Martinis for a special cocktail. The citrus flavors of the Cosmopolitans will pair very well with the flavors here.

Again, most items can be prepared in advance and kept chilled until serving.

Shopping List

Delicata Squash

4 Delicata squash

4 Tbls unsalted butter

2 Tbls olive oil (extra virgin not necessary but ok)

Salt and Pepper

1 bunch fresh thyme

Spiced Carrots

1 bag cleaned baby carrots

1 medium yellow onion

½ cup extra virgin olive oil

½ cup sugar

½ cup cider vinegar

1 tsp celery salt

¼ tsp dry yellow mustard

Salt

Mini Crab Cakes

1 pound lump crabmeat

2 large eggs

4 Tbls mayonnaise

1 small red bell pepper

1¼ tsp Old Bay Seasoning

¼ tsp cayenne pepper

1¼ tsp yellow mustard

1½ tsp fresh chopped parsley

8 Ritz crackers crumbled

Portobello Mushrooms Stuffed with Sausage

18 small portobello mushrooms

½ pound ground Italian sausage (either mild or hot)

1 small jar roasted red peppers or pimentos

1 bunch of fresh cilantro

1 garlic clove

5 Tbls dry white wine

½ cup dry bread crumbs

2 oz freshly grated Parmesan cheese

1 Tbls olive oil

½ stick unsalted butter

Puffed Pastry Parmesan Strips

1 sheet puff pastry dough

2 cups oil for deep frying

6 oz Parmesan cheese

Cosmopolitan Martinis

Vodka

Cointreau

Limes

Cranberry juice

Lemons for garnish (optional)

Baked Delicata Squash Rings

(Makes 16 to 20 pieces)
Recipe courtesy of Leslie McGrath

1. Preheat oven to 425 degrees Fahrenheit

2. Cut 4 Delicata Squash into ½ inch rounds, do not remove the rind, you should get 4 to 5 rounds per squash. (The rind of Delicata squash is totally edible)

3. Cut out the center of the squash containing the seeds

4. Place squash rounds on 2 baking trays not touching

5. Add 2 Tbls olive oil to 4 Tbls melted unsalted butter and mix

6. Pour the olive oil and butter mixture evenly over rings and turn so that both sides are coated.

7. Sprinkle one side lightly with salt and pepper

8. Bake for 15 to 20 minutes until rounds are golden brown but not totally limp. They should be tender when pierced with a fork but not squishy

9. Remove from oven and sprinkle with approximately 1 Tbls chopped fresh thyme

They can be served warm or at room temperature.

Spiced Carrots

(Makes 18 to 24 pieces)
Recipe courtesy of Weezie Morris

1. Bring 4 quarts of water to a boil and add 1 Tbls salt

2. Place 1 bag of cleaned baby carrots in boiling water and blanch for 5 minutes

3. Drain, but do not rinse, and place in large bowl

4. Thinly slice one medium yellow onion and add to the carrots

5. Place the following in a bowl and mix well

    a. $\frac{1}{2}$ cup extra virgin olive oil

    b. $\frac{1}{2}$ cup sugar

    c. $\frac{1}{2}$ cup cider vinegar

    d. 1 tsp celery salt

    e. $\frac{1}{4}$ tsp dry mustard

6. Pour the mixture over the carrots and onion and toss

7. Refrigerate at least 4 hours, but overnight is much better

Serve cold or at room temperature.

Mini Crab Cakes

(Makes 18 pieces)
From "Brunch On The Porch"

1. In a large bowl, whisk 2 large eggs until frothy

2. Add:

    a. 4 Tbls real mayonnaise

    b. 1 small red bell pepper, finely diced

    c. $1\frac{1}{4}$ tsp Old Bay Seasoning

    d. $\frac{1}{4}$ tsp cayenne pepper

    e. $1\frac{1}{4}$ tsp yellow mustard

    f. $1\frac{1}{2}$ tsp fresh chopped parsley

    g. 8 crumbled Ritz crackers

3. Check the crab meat for any shells and add to the egg mixture

4. Mix gently and let rest for about 15 minutes

5. Lightly dampen your hands and form the mixture into 18 mini cakes and place on wax paper. This can also be easily done by using a large tablespoon to scoop the mixture onto the wax paper.

6. Cover with another sheet of wax paper and flatten the crab cakes slightly

7. Refrigerate for at least 2 hours but 4 is better and overnight is ok. (If you skip this step, the crab cakes will not hold together when frying.)

8. Take from refrigerator 15 minutes before frying and bring to room temperature

9. Heat a large frying pan to medium high heat and add 1 Tbls olive oil. (Do not put cakes in pan before oil is hot.)

10. Fry cakes for 2 to 3 minutes per side, turning only once

Serve warm or at room temperature.

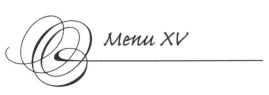

Portobello Mushrooms Stuffed with Sausage

(Makes 18 pieces)
From "Dinner On The Porch"

Preparation – Mushrooms

1. Preheat broiler

2. Remove stems from 18 small portobello mushrooms and save

3. Remove dark veins from the underside of the mushroom caps and discard

4. Wipe mushrooms with a paper towel or cloth to clean (do not rinse or use any water)

5. Place mushrooms cavity side down on broiler pan

6. Coat tops with 2 to 3 Tbls melted unsalted butter

7. Place under the broiler for about 3 minutes until soft but not collapsed

8. Remove and turn caps over for filling

Preparation – Stuffing

9. Place the following in a food processor and pulse until minced and set aside:

    a. 1 large clove of garlic (if using hot sausage, no garlic is required)

    b. 3 Tbls roasted peppers or pimentos

    c. 2 heaping Tbls cilantro

10. Chop the saved mushroom stems

11. Heat 1 Tbls olive oil in medium size skillet

12. Add ½ pound ground Italian sausage (either mild or hot) and the chopped mushroom stems to skillet and sauté until sausage is lightly cooked (just until red color is gone)

13. Add the mixture from the food processor and mix

14. Add ½ cup dry bread crumbs and mix

15. Add 3 to 5 Tbls dry white wine and mix (mixture should be damp but not sloshy)

16. Remove from heat

You can do this entire recipe up to this point in advance (up to one day) and refrigerate; but remove from refrigerator and bring to room temperature before baking.

Finish

1. Preheat oven to 375 degrees Fahrenheit

2. Place mushroom caps on baking sheet

3. Fill cavities to heaping with the stuffing

4. Sprinkle with 2 oz freshly grated Parmesan cheese

5. Bake for about 15 minutes until top of stuffing is brown

Serve warm or at room temperature.

Puff Pastry Parmesan Strips
(Makes 32 pieces)

1. Preheat 2 cups of oil in a deep fryer or deep sided skillet to 375 degrees Fahrenheit

2. Take 1 sheet of thawed puff pastry dough and place on floured surface

3. Cut dough into 4 equal long strips

4. Cut strips into 8 pieces each

5. Fry 8 pieces at a time for approximately 3 minutes or until golden brown

6. Drain on paper towels and sprinkle with 6 oz of freshly grated Parmesan cheese

7. Continue until all pieces are done

Serve warm or at room temperature.

Cosmopolitan Martini

(Per drink)

2 oz of really good Vodka (I like Absolut or Blue Ice)
½ ounce Cointreau
Juice of ½ lime
Splash of cranberry juice

1. Put all ingredients in a shaker.

2. Shake well and strain into a chilled martini glass.

3. Garnish with a twist of lemon (optional)

 # Wine

Tim recommends serving this menu with a light Italian red wine such as a Chianti or other Sangiovese. A Valpolicella would also work well.

Index of Recipes

Hors d'œuvres

Special Cocktails

Expressions of Gratitude

Throughout my life, I've been lucky enough to live and travel all over the world. I've been to every state in this country and lived in eight of them. While working for Petrofina, I lived in Montreal, Brussels, and Lichtenstein and had many extraordinary international travel experiences. I've climbed the pyramids in Egypt, been a guest of the Minister of Energy in Libya, fished for Arctic Char in the Arctic Circle, seen the Tar Sands in Calgary, studied at Le Cordon Bleu in Paris, and eaten Peking Duck in Hong Kong. It's all been wonderful, but no matter where I've been, every summer, I always come home to the little cottage on Crystal Lake.

Crystal Lake has been the one constant in my life; my spiritual home. This little cottage is where I wrap myself in the warmth and comfort of family and lifelong friends; where I can feel the presence of past generations; where I come to renew my soul. My memories are a rich blend of long summer days filled with swimming, bike rides, water skiing, sailing, walks on the beach, drive-in movies, and gatherings by the fireplace. This is where my youth is stored. When I'm away, I miss seeing the water's surface sparkle and flash as the sun rises over the lake; the smell of the pine trees after a summer rain; the pungent earthy flavor of the morel mushrooms; but mostly I miss the feeling of joy brought on by the laughter of those I care for.

As time continues to pick up speed and I come to realize how short the journey really is, I'm grateful that I recognize and savor the joy, and hopeful that I return some to those who travel with me along the way.

Party Notes

Party Notes

_____

_____

_____

_____

_____

_____

_____

_____

_____

_____

_____

_____

_____

_____

_____

_____